AUTHENTIC POWER

Principles, Strategies & Tools for Achieving Full Human Potential

AUTHENTIC POWER

Principles, Strategies & Tools for Achieving Full Human Potential

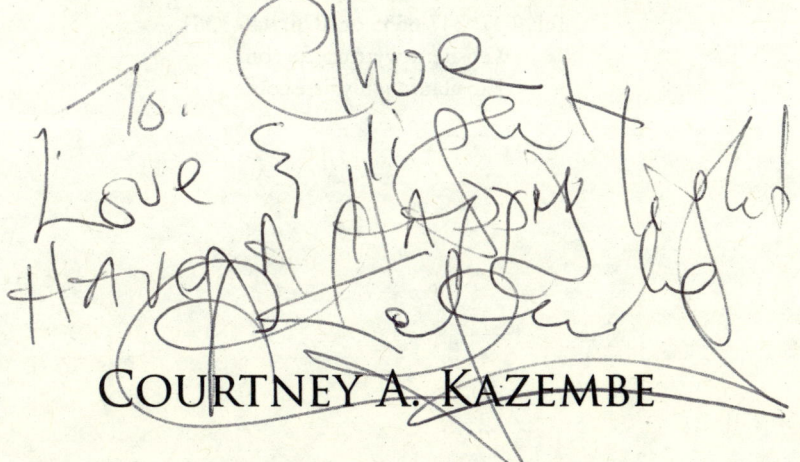

Courtney A. Kazembe

Global Institute for Freedom, Transformation and Enlightenment (GIFTE)

Copyright © 2009 by Courtney A. Kazembe

All rights reserved including the right of reproduction in whole or in part in any form.

No part of this book may be reproduced, stored in a retrieval system, or transmitted by any means, electronic, mechanical, photocopying, recording, or otherwise, without written permission from the author or publisher. There is one exception. Brief passages may be quoted in articles or reviews.

Library and Archives Canada Cataloguing in Publication

CIP data on file with the National Library and Archives

ISBN 978-1-926582-36-8

For information or free catalog, contact:
Global Institute for Freedom, Transformation and Enlightenment
(GIFTE)
Tel: (647) 347-6535 or (876) 946-1361
Website: www.mygifte.com
Email:info@mygifte.com

ACKNOWLEDGMENTS

I gratefully acknowledge and express my love and appreciation to the many wonderful people who have made this project possible:

To all my teachers through whose lives and writings has come the wisdom of the ages. I have learned from your legacy.

To all my colleagues, clients, and seminar participants whose deep sharing and synergy have moved me many levels beyond my own thinking, you have taught me so much.

To all who have read parts of this manuscript and contributed their insights and wisdom I am grateful.

Love and light.

CONTENTS

Foreword 1   9

Part I INTRODUCTION
1. Change   15
2. Attitude   20
3. Persistence   28

Part II PRINCIPLES
4. New Paradigms   35
5. Integrity   46
6. Responsibility   53
7. Challenges   60
8. Discipline   69

Part III THE MENTAL
9. The Conscious Mind   79
10. The Subconscious Mind   86
11. The Superconscious Mind   94
12. The Law of Thinking   105

Part IV THE EMOTIONAL
13. The Nature of Emotions   117
14. The Inner Child   134
15. Overcoming Our Fears   145
16. Interdependence   154

Part V THE SPIRITUAL
17. The Nature of Existence   169
18. The Nature of the Soul   182
19. The Nature of God   194

Part VI OUR HUMAN POTENTIAL

20. Love — 207
21. Power — 219
22. Purpose — 227
23. Prosperity — 242

FOREWORD

This book is about a very special type of power – Authentic Power. It is infinite in its supply and is available to everyone in infinite proportions. Authentic Power is an exploration of what it is to be human and how to achieve that incredible potential.

What is power? Power is simply the ability to produce the results we want in our lives. It is what everyone wants and no one seems to have enough of. World leaders, housewives, business executives, lovers – all are in search of that which will enable them to achieve their desired goals. Without power we would accomplish nothing.

The question is, How can we get more power? or more precisely, How can we become connected to the infinite supply of power? To understand this we must first understand how power works. Power operates under the same principle as love. The more one gives to others the more one receives in return. Unfortunately many of us assume that there is a limited supply of power; that giving power to another means diminishing ones own power.

This book tells how we can achieve ultimate power by becoming connected to the universal supply of power and by giving power to everyone in our lives. It shows how we can unleash the vast storehouse of human potential that is untapped virtually everywhere in our lives. The secret of achieving success in our lives lies in learning how to release this hidden potential.

The goal of this book is to help us become self-actualized, to realize our individual human potential for meaningful work and for loving relationships with others.

This book's purpose is to inspire you to live the life which perhaps, until now you have only imagined for yourself. Its mission is to give you the tools to create that life so that no matter the obstacles along the way, you know you have what it takes to surmount them. It is a quest for insight, wholeness and integrity. We shall embark upon a journey to discover what it is to be human.

This book helps us address both the frustrations in the fulfillment of our personal lives and the limitations that prevent our spiritual awakening. Why don't I do a better job of creating the kind of life that I think I want? Why are some aspects of my life so hard to change?

Authentic power provides a way to work with ourselves fully as we are now, and to work with whatever it is in us that blocks our personal and spiritual development. We need maps of the psyche that do not idealize or gloss over our human failings. Authentic power outlines a map of human consciousness that includes our devils as well as our angels, the vulnerable child as well as the competent adult, the petty ego as well as the grand visionary longings.

The practice of honest, compassionate confrontation with our lower selves, while anchoring ourselves more and more solidly in the higher self, brings the greatest personal liberation. This is a path of empowerment through self-responsibility.

Each of us has something special about us. Each of us has a unique vision, a meaning and purpose to our life, with which we can be the most successful, the most fulfilled, and the happiest. The discovery and fulfillment of that unique vision is our life's purpose and will bring with it our highest spiritual and material fulfillment.

Authentic Power reveals how to contact, communicate, and work with the highest spiritual power and how to make that power available for the spiritual and material transformation of the individual, and through the individual, the world.

Authentic Power helps us to purify ourselves so that we can become conscious, self-realized people, and learn to love in the true sense of the word. As members of society our task is to transform our surroundings and planet earth, and create a global community of brother-sisterhood through the spreading of the new consciousness and developing new paradigms and ways of communication, and discovering new methods of problem solving.

Becoming conscious co-creators of new paradigms and reality is the most joyful and positive aim of this work. May this work touch you deeply, not only in your mind, but also in your heart. May it inspire you. May love's blessings be showered upon you and overflow into every life you touch.

Peace, Love, Light and Prosperity.

Courtney Akinwale Kazembe

PART I

INTRODUCTION

Change
Attitude
Persistence

CHAPTER 1

CHANGE

*If we always do what we have always done
we will always get what we have always got.*

One of the things that strikes me the most about human beings, is the extent to which we will all go to avoid change and the unknown. We seem almost paralyzed when it comes to venturing out on our own, or starting something new, such as a new job or a new project. For example, we all know that many of our institutions and our habits do not work and yet we are reluctant to change them. Furthermore, in our personal, social, religious and economic lives many of our rituals and norms remain ineffective and antiquated. Do we even think of change? How does change and transformation come about? Why do we resist change so much? We must come to the realization that unless we embrace change, in essence we remain slaves to our past.

Over the last decade, I have been investigating this area of human development and attitudinal change. This inquiry has led me into a study of why we vehemently resist change and through that resistance ultimately resist freedom. It occurred to me that human beings in general tend to stick with the familiar, no matter how bad it is, rather than risking the unknown however promising it may potentially be. We resign ourselves to the familiar, saying, "it is not so bad" and hide from venturing out into the unknown.

This predicament is a result of the way our minds work.

Once we have been inculcated into a particular tribe, the particulars of that tribe such as its religion, culture or way of seeing the world, becomes the model for how we live our lives. For example, if a woman was born and raised in the West, she will find it relatively easier to take off most of her clothes and go to the beach, than if she was born and raised in the Middle East. This has to do with the culture in which one was inculcated. The world occurs to us in a particular way depending on this framework, and as long as we stick to it our results are limited by this particular frame of reference.

This process is interesting, because most of our frameworks today are incongruent with the evolution of universal principles, such as prosperity, abundance, freedom, trust and love. These are the fundamental principles that underpin the functioning of the universe. The opposites of universal principles are fear and illusion. When our beliefs, assumptions and actions are out of alignment with these principles, our lives become chaotic and impoverished and we live in a world of illusion and fear.

This begs the question: "If the old framework is so bad, why are we sticking with it?" I believe that our inability to welcome change lies in ignorance, fear and in our human unwillingness to face the unknown. As human beings we have an incredible ability to cope with any circumstances. It seems as if once we have become accustomed to one particular set of circumstances — even if we don't like them – we are reluctant to change them. The process is called homeostasis and it means that we move towards a relatively stable state of equilibrium. For example, a slave could have a relatively stable state of equilibrium under slavery and resist any attempts to end slavery. In fact many slaves were strongly against any attempts to end slavery. Likewise today, we are resisting all attempts to free our body, heart, mind, and soul.

If we are going to solve our personal and community

problems, we need to develop the necessary knowledge and courage that will support us while we step outside of familiar ground and venture into uncharted territory. We must understand that "if we always do what we've always done, we will always get what we've always got". In other words, our current status is the consequence of operating in our comfort zone, and as long as we continue to operate within this framework, we can expect to get only more of the same. It is insane to continue to do the same things year after year and generation after generation and yet expect different results.

As long as we are consistently sticking to dis-empowering frameworks — those frameworks will limit anything we do. We might work on our behavior, try harder, be more diligent, double our speed, elect a new politician or a new pastor — our efforts will only give more of the same or get us to the wrong place faster.

Our frameworks operate like a road map. If I want to go north and I am heading south it does not matter how fast I drive or what time saving mechanism I employ, fundamentally I am going in the wrong direction. Also it does not matter how fast I climb the ladder – if the ladder, is leaning against the wrong wall, I will end up in the wrong place. Maybe our fundamental problems have less to do with our situations and circumstances and more to do with having dis-empowering frameworks.

If we desire different results, we will not only have to do things differently but more importantly we will have to do different things. We will have to be prepared to change our framework, paradigms and belief systems. We will have to invent new ways of being and doing. And although this is actually easy, very few of us are brave enough to try it, because of our fear of the unknown.

I am reminded of an old Middle Eastern story of a spy who was captured and sentenced to death by a general of the

Persian Army. The general had fallen upon a strange and rather bizarre custom. He would permit the condemned person to make a choice – to either face the firing squad or pass through the black door.

As the moment of execution drew near, the general ordered the spy to be brought before him for a short, final interview, the primary purpose of which was to receive the doomed man's answer to the question: "Which shall it be, the firing squad or the Black Door?" It was not an easy question, and the prisoner hesitated, but soon made it known that he much preferred the firing squad. Not long thereafter a volley of shots rang out in the courtyard announcing that the grim sentence had been carried out.

The general, staring at his boots, turned to his aide and said, "You see how it is with human beings, they will always prefer the known to the unknown. It is characteristic of people to be afraid of the undefined, and yet I gave him a choice."

"What lies behind the Black Door?" Asked the aide.

"Freedom," replied the general, "and I have known only a few persons brave enough to take it."

Like so many stories out of the East, this one carries a very strong message that we will often choose the familiar, even if it is undesirable, over the unknown that might be a wonderful opportunity. Few people are brave enough to choose freedom even if they recognize it as freedom, because they are stuck in their state of relative stability and equilibrium, even when it is highly undesirable.

When you read the story about "the Black Door," you probably said to yourself, "I would have chosen the Black Door. I would have nothing to lose, the firing squad was certain death." And most of us would say the same thing. But actually faced with the choice, would you, really? How many doors to freedom have we passed up during our lifetime because we cling so fiercely to the familiar? How many times have events come about that have caused you to worry about them? You may have even thought the events were calamities at the time, and later they proved to be blessings in disguise. Consider each of these events, as a Black Door through which you passed to greater freedom. Consider this in light of the fact that at the time you would probably have chosen to keep things, as they were if you had been given the choice. What a mistake that would have been!

It is essential to remember, if we can, that it is those very things that we worry about and fear the most that turn out to be great opportunities.

I am further reminded of the Jamaican reggae artiste Bob Marley's song "emancipate yourself from mental slavery, none but ourselves can free our minds." If we would only learn how to free our minds we would experience life as bliss, abundance and joy. We would be prepared to see challenges, and changes as opportunities for renewal and growth.

It is fear and contraction of the mind that keep us in physical, emotional, intellectual and spiritual bondage and poverty. And no one but ourselves can liberate us from this captivity.

When we break out of this fear and contraction, we experience what is called transformation and empowerment. It is metaphorically a cocoon transforming into a beautiful and magnificent butterfly, with the freedom to be. It is only at this stage that we begin to experience the magnificence and divinity of what it really means to be human.

CHAPTER 2

ATTITUDE

The stuff that makes the difference

Attitude is the way we see and respond to life. It is our physical, mental, emotional and spiritual approach, disposition and posture towards life. Instilling the right approach, disposition and posture towards life is fundamental to the work and study we are undertaking in this book. When everything is taken away from us, the right attitude alone can carry us through.

Your attitude is the way you think about your life and all it contains. It is your approach and perspective on life. It influences your actions and reactions. It affects your relationship with others and your relationship with your self. Because your attitude reflects your thinking, it is the beginning point of creation and possibility. They are first and foremost the residents of your mind and both of them are released by your attitude. People who soar have the courage to insist on positive attitudes in their life. They understand that life offers many surprises, but believe that within those surprises are lessons and that from the lessons, come the wisdom.

The more I study human development and empowerment, the more I appreciate the importance of having the right attitude towards life. Attitude is one of the most important tools towards self-actualization and self-empowerment. It is even more important than money, knowledge and education. It is also more important than giftedness, appearance and skill. Attitude can single- handedly make or break a person, a team, a church, an organization, a home or a relationship. It is also the single most important factor in interpersonal relationships.

The essential thing about attitude is for us to understand that we have a choice each day about the attitude we will embrace for that day. Further, we have a choice about every situation and circumstance in our lives. We can choose to give an empowering interpretation to occurrences, or on the other hand, we can choose to give them a dis-empowering interpretation. The problem is that we are programmed in cultures that have pre-conceived interpretations for many situations. We then react to situations and circumstances without giving them conscious thought. The challenge for us is to find new interpretations that empower us rather than dis-empower us.

In life misfortunes happen. It is not what happens to us, but how we deal with what happens that makes the difference. Most of the unfortunate circumstances in our lives potentially have an advantage hidden in them. Life can be seen as an up and down ride. Most of us only want to experience the ups, so we go around complaining about the downs, not realizing that the downs can be "blessings in disguise". Therefore we should not run from the challenges in life, but rather face them with eagerness to receive the message they bring.

I am convinced that my life is ten percent of what happens to me, and ninety percent how I react to it. Most of us live our lives on automatic pilot. We never seem to make the appropriate response to the challenges that life has to offer. We must realize that "if we always do what we have always done we will always get what we have always got."

While we cannot change our past and the fact that people will act in a certain way, and we cannot change the inevitable, what we can do, however, is play the only string we have, and that is, our attitude toward life. In the story told by Victor Frankl in his book *Man's Search for Meaning* about people in a Nazi concentration camp, Frankl wrote:

"We who lived in concentration camps can remember the men who walked through the huts comforting others, giving away their last piece of bread. They may have been few in number, but they offer sufficient proof that everything can be taken from a man but one thing: the last of human freedoms — to choose one's attitude in any given set of circumstances, to choose one's own way.

And there were always choices to make. Every day, every hour, offered the opportunity to make a decision, a decision which determined whether you would or would not submit to those powers which threatened to rob you of your very self, your inner freedom; which determined whether or not you would become the plaything of circumstance."

Attitude is such an important thing that we cannot leave it up to chance. We must keep a conscious moment by moment watch on our attitude. We must make an effort to implement regimens and practices which will assist us in having the right attitude in our daily lives. These will include first of all, having the right people in our lives. If we want to have a great attitude about life, we must associate with people who possess great attitudes. I often tell people that seventy five percent of their success, happiness and peace of mind depend on who they marry. If you marry someone with a positive attitude it will rub off on you. If on the other hand, you marry someone with a negative attitude it will equally rub off on you.

I marvel about the incredible attitude Nelson Mandela must have had to survive twenty-seven years in a South

African prison. And after all that punishment and suffering, he emerged as his nation's leader with the tenacity and loving nature to forgive his persecutors. Attitude is like that — if you maintain a positive attitude and have some patience, your goals and dreams will be realized.

The easiest way to maintain a positive attitude is to discover your purpose in life and endeavor to accomplish it. One has to be willing to engage in an ongoing practice towards a worthy cause with a positive attitude, if one wants to lead a successful life.

A positive attitude requires courage, because it is the decision not to be defeated no matter what challenge is present. What is truly magnificent is the person who no matter what card of life he or she has been dealt still wins because the game is played with acceptance, intelligence, wit, humor and integrity. If we could only let go of our fears, then our spirits would be triumphant over that which could disable us from flying through life at the full range of our capacities.

A positive attitude does not dissolve life's problems. Rather it is an effective and constructive approach to dealing with them. The positive thinker accepts life as it unfolds without trying to control it or having to conform to limited human expectations. The positive thinker regards life as an adventure where the rewards are in the risk and the pleasure is in responding to the challenges. A positive attitude is good insurance for life. Whether life is privileged or painful has nothing to do with our circumstances or our situations. It is a direct reflection of our attitude. As difficult, painful and unpredictable as life can be it cannot defeat us, unless we choose to be defeated. You need only take charge of your thoughts and you can do what you will with them. This is not being out of touch with reality — this is courage. It is also the only way you can afford to think, if you are to manifest the vision you have for your life.

I would like to share with you the following seven principles for attitudinal healing. If you choose to take these principles seriously and follow them on a daily basis, you will be surprised to see your goals magically realized before your eyes.

Seven Principles of Attitudinal Healing

1. Love

The essence of our being is love. There is no energy more powerful than love. As you learn to love you are bringing into your life the most potent force in the universe. Love creates miracles, heals all wounds, and purifies all lower energies. You cannot lose by giving love away, for the more you give, the more you receive in return. When you choose love you bring about the highest good for yourself and others. Offering love is always the right choice. With love you can transform, purify, neutralize, lift, expand, connect, harmonize, balance, amplify, magnetize, accept, and add light and beauty to all the energy around you. With love you can transform or be transparent to people's emotions and thoughts, neutralize "negative" energy, and harmonize with all life in the universe. Importantly, since love is eternal, we need not see death as fearful, but a transition from one stage to another. We can also choose and direct ourselves to perceive others as either extending love or giving a call for help. All energy in the universe responds positively to love. Therefore, we need only love. LOVE! LOVE! LOVE!

2. Release:

Health is inner peace. Healing is releasing and letting go. Most of us have blockages in our physical, emotional and mental bodies that cause disease, discomfort and pain. We hold on to most of these blockages unconsciously. We then get stuck in a rut and even when we cure the physical illnesses sometimes we do not heal and the illness comes back in the same form or even in a different form. True healing only occurs when one's spirit releases negative thoughts and emotions towards oneself and others. We must choose and direct ourselves to be peaceful inside, regardless of what is happening outside.

3. Giving and Receiving:

Giving and receiving are the same. We are continually drawing into our lives what we give and expect.

Whether we attract good or bad, it is governed by the same principle. You have probably made the remark, "Oh, yes, it is just as I expected." And especially when some unpleasant condition or circumstance arose. You invited the condition just because you gave out the thought of expecting it. You can also expect good to appear on the same principle and you can help it to come to pass by the method of your preparation. Many failures occur because we do not force our expectation to keep apace with our desires. Very often we desire one thing and expect in our hearts another, which creates confusion. When a mind is confused, there is no cooperation, nor is there the united strength to attract the force it requires. Positive mental radiation will drive away all clouds of doubt and fear with confident expectation that all things will work all right. You operate a law that can and will put all things right. There is a power within, greater by far than any difficulty that you can ever meet; that power will never fail to see us through.

4. Live In The Moment:

Let go of the past and the future and live fully in the moment. Live in appreciation and gratitude. Invite change into your life, if only through your attitude. And remind yourself continually of the message of all spiritual masters worth their salt. Keep your spirit in the present time. Jesus said, "Leave the dead and get on with life" and "let the dead bury the dead." And Buddha said, "There is only now." Now is the only time there is and each instant is for giving and loving. When we live in the moment we get to experience each person, situation or event as new, without coloration from the past. In order to live in the moment we must be conscious, aware and alert. When we are not living consciously we are then led by our subconscious memory and we live from our history. When we live subconsciously, we have an attitude by default. On the other hand when we live consciously we have an attitude by design.

5. Forgive:

Learn to love yourself and others by forgiving rather than judging and blaming. Forgiveness is not the same as telling the other person who harms you, "it is okay," "I forgive you" which is more or less the way most people view it. Rather, forgiveness is a complex act of consciousness, one that liberates the psyche and soul from the need for personal vengeance and the perception of oneself as a victim. More than releasing from blame the people who caused our wounds, forgiveness means releasing the control that the perception of victimhood has over our psyches. In fact when we forgive the other we are actually doing ourselves a bigger favor. The liberation that forgiveness generates comes in the transition to higher state of consciousness – not just in theory, but energetically, psychologically and biologically. In fact the consequence of a genuine act of forgiveness borders on the miraculous.

6. Gratitude:

In everything give thanks. Gratitude is a powerful space to be in. Gratitude is a state of thankfulness and appreciation for life and the entire universe. When we operate from this state of consciousness, we assume a positive attitude and demeanor. We can be grateful and appreciative of everyone in our life, because everyone is in our life to teach us something.

Even our perceived enemies are in our lives to teach us something. Likewise, every event, situation and circumstance occurs in our lives to teach us a lesson. Therefore we can be in a state of perpetual gratefulness.

7. Acceptance:

Acceptance of your circumstances and situations as they are is one of the most important ways of maintaining a good attitude. Most of us go through life whining and complaining about situations, circumstances and events in our life. Living this way totally dis-empowers us and causes frustration and disappointment. Accepting life as it is — is wanting what you have in your life, as opposed to trying to satisfy an insatiable appetite. If we go through life, fighting, opposing, resisting, arguing, we are bound to meet with many obstacles and are likely to become so occupied fighting them that we lose sight of our real objective. The power of acceptance is not to fight the obstacles but to bless them and move on. Jesus said: "love your enemies; bless them that curse you, do good to them that hate you; pray for them that despitefully use you." To extend a loving thought, feeling or action to anyone or anything removes the opposition and enmity that once seemed there. This removal must first be in your consciousness. Once the thought of enmity is removed from your consciousness you will not attract the same condition again.

CHAPTER 3

PERSISTENCE

*Persistence is key to achieving
your full human potential.*

If you want to succeed in life, the first thing you have to do is discover your purpose in life. The second thing is to persist in that endeavor until you succeed. If you look at great persons who have accomplished their purpose, you will find one thing, which is consistent in all of them. They persisted through major trials and tribulations, until they succeeded. No matter what obstacles came in their way, they never gave up.

I believe that most of us give up too easily on our dreams. Some of us believe that we should try once, if that much, at our dreams and then fall back to mediocrity.

Each one of us was born with a purpose. Something unique and special, that we came here to do. No one else can do this for us, this dream or purpose was given to us. However, we only get to achieve this purpose when we persist and overcome whatever is in the way.

TRY, TRY & TRY: YOU WILL SUCCEED AT LAST

I like one of Jimmy Cliff's songs that goes like this, "You can get it if you really want it, but you must try, try and try, you will succeed at last." I think Jimmy Cliff knew what he was talking about. Any one, who has achieved any level of success, will tell you the same thing. The only question is "Do you really want it?" If you really want it and you try and try then you will surely get it.

In the Orient, young bulls are tested for the fight arena in a certain manner. Each is brought to the ring and allowed to attack a picador who pricks them with a lance. The bravery of each bull is then rated with care according to the number of times he demonstrates his willingness to charge in spite of the sting of the blade. Life is kind of like that, each day we are tested in like manner. If we persist, if we continue to charge forward, we will succeed.

Let's take the story of Alex Haley for example. For eight long years, this struggling young writer wrote incredible numbers of short stories and articles for publication, and for eight long years, they were rejected. Fortunately, he did not give up, and the world will always be grateful.

Alex Haley spent most of his time in the Navy, writing routine reports and letters. He learned how to say things eloquently, yet concisely. After his hitch in the Navy, he tried desperately to make it as a writer, but despite those eight years and hundreds of stories and articles, he was unable to sell even one.

Once, however, an editor did write an encouraging note on the rejection slip. It simply said, "Nice try."

I think you will agree that most of us would not rate that high on the encouragement list, but it brought tears to the young writer's eye and he was given new hope and he continued to persist. He just would not give up.

Finally, after many years, he wrote a book that deeply affected the entire world and helped him to become one of the most influential writers of the 1970s. I'm speaking of his book "Roots", which was made into one of the most-watched television mini-series of all time.

The message is clear: If you have a dream and if you believe you have some ability that can be expressed, don't give up. Who knows, maybe on your next effort, somebody will say "Nice Try." That might be all the encouragement you'll need. Remember that success might be just around the corner, over the next hill, or at the end of that next effort. Think about it, give it a try and I'll see you at the top.

Play Everything at 100%

We must also develop the habit of playing everything at a hundred percent. It makes life more meaningful and fun. Holding back, not playing at a hundred percent, will keep you from your goal. To the extent that you don't play at a hundred percent, you set up blocks from playing at a hundred percent. And those obstructions prevent your success. For each moment that you don't play at a hundred percent, what happens? You create a lot of barriers, which are not conducive to having what you want. So play at one hundred percent. The universe supports those who play at one hundred percent. Only then can you become the true person you were meant to be and accomplish your purpose in life.

Complete Whatever You Start

A major source of negative energy in your life stems from the incomplete things in your life. When you start something and fail to complete it — it is not only a source of great disappointment, but it also robs you of your mental, physical emotional and spiritual energy. You make a withdrawal from your integrity account. When you complete something — something else gets added onto you more than that which you completed. It is therefore very important, that you endeavor to complete whatever you start.

I remember a saying oft repeated by my high school math teacher, "If a task is once begun never leave it until it is done – be it a labor great or small, do it well or not at all." All those things that are incomplete rob you of the power and energy to have what you want. You must aim to be complete at all times.

We all have challenges. And chances are there is something that is going to take everything out of us to accomplish it. Such a challenge is worthy of us. In order to be a success at this challenge we will have to stretch, probably do something new to our soul.

While your soul is excited about its challenge in this lifetime, there are other parts of you that are afraid and want to resist challenges. These parts of you will come up with all sorts of excuses why you shouldn't start or persist with your purpose. If you succumb to this part of you, then you will lose your personal power and you will wither away and live your life like a zombie until you die.

If however you find enough personal power to persist through tough times, through abandonment, through pain, through tiredness, through physical, mental and emotional exhaustion, then you will accomplish your objectives. And you would have experienced the true joy in life.

One of the most critical things to remember about persistence is that, most of the time we quit just before the breakthrough. In fact the phrase "it is always darkest just before dawn" is true most of the time. It is almost always that time when we think we have nothing left that we should push on with determination and resolution.

Life is like a school. We have to persist through all of the lessons and challenges; otherwise we get stuck and cannot move on to the next stage. When we don't persist through our challenges, it is kind of like getting stuck in the fifth grade and staying there all of our lives. Life then becomes boring and predictable.

The gems of life are not necessarily at the beginning of the journey, it can be found on every step of the way and the major reward is in finishing what you started. We must exercise our personal power and persist until we accomplish our purpose.

PART II

PRINCIPLES

New Paradigms
Integrity
Responsibility
Challenges
Discipline

CHAPTER 4

NEW PARADIGMS

Breakthrough performance is predicated not on doing better or more in the existing paradigms but on breaking up those old paradigms and creating new ones.

Before we can understand how to solve our primary problems, we need to understand our own "paradigms" and how to make a "paradigm shift". The word paradigm comes from the ancient Greek word *paradeigma*, meaning pattern, or framework of thought. It was originally a scientific term, and is more commonly used today to mean a model, theory, perception, assumption, or frame of reference. In the more general sense, it's the way we "see" the world — not in terms of our visual sense of sight, but in terms of perceiving, understanding and interpreting. A paradigm is a scheme for understanding and explaining certain aspects of our reality.

A paradigm is the basic way of perceiving, thinking, valuing, and doing, associated with a particular vision of reality. A dominant paradigm is seldom, if ever, stated explicitly; it exists as an unquestioned, tacit understanding that is transmitted through culture and to succeeding generations through direct experience, rather than being taught.

For our purpose, a simple way to understand paradigms is to see them as maps or blueprints. The map is not the territory and neither is the blueprint the building. A map is simply an explanation of certain aspects of the territory. The blueprint or plan is simply an explanation of how the building is to be built. That's exactly what a paradigm is. It is a theory, an explanation, or model of something else.

Suppose for example, I was going to visit my friend in New York City. A street map would be of great help to me in reaching my destination. But suppose I purchased a map that was incorrectly labeled. The map was labeled New York City, but was in fact a map of Los Angeles. Can you imagine the frustration, the ineffectiveness of trying to reach my destination? As long as I stuck to the wrong map, anywhere I go would be the wrong place. Even if I found fun and enjoyment, I would still be in the wrong place. This is similar to having the wrong paradigm. With the wrong paradigm you can actually be sabotaging yourself, without even recognizing that you are doing so.

More importantly, there is just no right way of doing the wrong thing. As long as you are consistently sticking to the wrong paradigm — that map will limit anything you do. You might work on your behavior — you could try harder, be more diligent, double your speed — but your effort would only assist in getting you, to the wrong place faster. When you get to the wrong place, even if you think you like it, the point is you would still be lost. Our fundamental problems have less to do with our situation and circumstances and more to do with having the wrong paradigms.

If I have the right map of New York City, then diligence becomes important, and when I encounter frustrating obstacles along the way, then attitudes can make a real difference. Also if I have the right map, then the terrain, a luxury car and money in my pocket make a big difference. But the first and most important requirements are the right maps, blueprints or frame of reference — paradigms. It is crucial that we become aware of the paradigms in our lives and develop a mechanism to shift to the right paradigms — the paradigms that will empower us and lead us to our desired result.

We all have many paradigms. These can be divided into two main categories: first, there are paradigms of the way things are, our realities, and secondly, there are paradigms of the way things should be, our values. We interpret everything we experience through these mental pictures. We seldom question their accuracy; we're usually unaware that we have them, and are therefore unaware of the effect they have on our lives. We simply assume that the way we see things, is the way they really are, or the way they ought to be. We are inculcated into these paradigms. Some of them are centuries old. If we would just take the time to examine them, we would soon find out how inappropriate some of these paradigms are.

Another way to think about paradigms is as games. All games have boundaries and rules. For example if we are playing chess there is a boundary — the chess board. There are rules about how to move the pieces. For me to be successful at chess, I must know the boundaries, the rules and the objectives of the game. It is also important to know the history of the game and who sets the rules and regulations of the game. If we can extend ourselves to see life as a big game, then it may give us some freedom about understanding our paradigm and may give us the power to start playing a different game.

Conditioning and culturalization powerfully affect our perceptions and our paradigms. Most of us have been inculcated in a paradigm of reality which invalidates many aspects of our existence. Various forces have combined to affect our perceptions and our paradigms. The institutions in our lives: society, schools, churches and other places of worship — all have made their silent unconscious impact on us and help shape our frame of reference, our maps and our games — our paradigms.

Each of us tends to think we see things as they are, that we are objective. We see the world, not as it is, but as we are

— or, as we have been conditioned to see it. When we open our mouths to describe what we see, we in effect describe ourselves, our perceptions, and our belief systems — our paradigms. The more aware we are of our basic paradigms, and the extent to which they influence our lives, the more we can take responsibility for those paradigms, examine them, test them against reality, and become empowered to change them.

THE PARADIGM EFFECT

Paradigms act as psychological filters — we literally see the world through our paradigms. What we can and cannot do; what we can and cannot see; what we can and cannot believe; who we can and cannot be; what is possible or impossible, are all limited and shaped by our paradigms. The effect of a paradigm is therefore like a box. We can go this far but no further. Everything that is possible is within that box. Any data that exists in the real world that does not fit our paradigm will have a difficult time getting through our filters. We will see little if any of it. Moreover, the data that does fit our paradigm, not only makes it through the filter, but is concentrated by the filtering process, thus creating an illusion of even greater support for the existing paradigm.

We see best what is consistent with our belief system — we see what is inside our box. We see poorly, or not at all, that which does not fit into our operating paradigm. When inconsistent data turns up we will either ignore it, or we will distort it until it fits our prevailing paradigm.

Our perception is dramatically determined by our paradigms. What may be perfectly visible and obvious to one person with one paradigm may quite literally be invisible to another person, with a different paradigm. We often speak about certain results being impossible. When we are convinced about the impossibility of a certain result, we should translate that to say — "Based on the paradigm I am practicing right now, I don't know how to achieve that result."

The paradigm effect can be seen in all areas of life. History has numerous examples. For centuries people believed that the earth was flat. Even when they were met with overwhelming information to the contrary, people still held on to the inaccurate paradigm. The paradigm effect impacts most significantly those who have the greatest investments in that particular paradigm.

Paradigm effects trap us in a world of limited possibility. We must become aware of how much influence our paradigms exert on our perception of the world around us. To improve our ability to anticipate and innovate, we must understand and appreciate the paradigm effect. To see the future more clearly, we must put aside the certainties of our present paradigms and begin to examine the uncertainties of new paradigms. By understanding the paradigm effect, we can begin to lift ourselves above its power to blind and trap us in a state of oblivion and begin to search for new possibilities, which will shape our future proactively and affirmatively.

Paradigm Paralysis

We have the tendency to get stuck into one particular paradigm, even when it has long out-lived its usefulness. Once we believe there is only one paradigm, any alternative possibility has to be wrong. Most people are stuck in a particular paradigm of reality. In fact, society over the years, insisted on advocating one paradigm and would literally kill anyone who deviated from it. This kind of rigid adherence to a particular paradigm, is what is referred to as paradigm paralysis.

On one of my visits to a southern Baptist church, the minister was enthusiastically preaching and saying that even if God should tell him that he was practicing and preaching the wrong things, he would not change. This is a classical example of paradigm paralysis. This preacher was so stuck to his belief system, that if he was to be presented with overwhelming evidence – even if God himself were to tell him otherwise, he would not change. He had so much invested in one paradigm, that he was willfully blind to any possibility of experiencing or shifting to a new paradigm.

It is very easy to develop paradigm paralysis — that is, the inability to shift paradigms. The more one has invested in a particular paradigm, the more likely it is for one to develop paradigm paralysis. New paradigms, put everyone practicing the old paradigm at great risk. The higher ones position, the greater the risk. The better you are at one paradigm and the more you have invested in it, the more you have to lose by changing paradigms. This is so because the new paradigm brings a new game, with new rules and everyone has to learn them anew.

The Power of a Paradigm Shift

New ideas and perspectives have the power to give birth to a new historic age. A paradigm shift is a distinctively new way of seeing and thinking about old problems. Almost every significant breakthrough in the field of scientific endeavor is first a break with tradition and with old ways of seeing and thinking of the problem.

For example, for more than four centuries, leading thinkers assumed that Ptolemy's paradigm of an earth centered universe was correct. Then Copernicus began seeing and thinking of the problem in a new way. He created a paradigm shift, by placing the sun at the center of the solar system. Everything took on a different interpretation. This brought about a great deal of resistance and persecution from those who had a lot invested in the old Ptolemy's paradigm.

Isaac Newton's model of physics, was a clockwork paradigm with predictable mechanical forces. But as scientists worked toward the elusive ultimate answers, bits of data here and there refused to fit into Newton's scheme. This is typical of any paradigm. Eventually, too many puzzling observations pile up outside the old framework of explanation and strain it. Usually at the point of crisis, someone has a new idea and begins to see and think of the problem in new ways. A powerful new insight explains the apparent contradictions. It introduces a new principle, a new perspective — a new paradigm.

Then entered Einstein with a new concept of how the universe works. The scientific world was revolutionized by the Einsteinian paradigm of relativity. It resolved much unfinished business, anomalies and riddles, which would not fit into the old physics. And it was a stunning alternative: The old mechanical rules of Newton were not universal, they did not hold at the level of galaxies. Our understanding of nature shifted from a Newtonian clockwork paradigm, to an Einsteinian uncertainty paradigm — from the absolute to the relative.

Einstein's laws can no longer solve all the problems we now face. No matter how many scientists attempted to fit all the existing data into the old paradigm, it did not work. Now there is a new player on the block — Stephen Hawking, introducing new concepts of time and new attempts at explaining the origins of the universe.

A new paradigm involves a principle that was present all along, but unknown to us. For example, the earth was never flat, but people for centuries lived out of a flat earth paradigm. New paradigms usually include the old as a partial truth, one aspect of how things work, while allowing for things to work in other ways as well. The new paradigm does more than the old. It predicts more accurately, and it throws open doors and windows for new explorations.

Given the superior power, scope and accuracy of the new paradigm, we might expect it to prevail rather quickly, but that does not usually happen. The problem is that we cannot embrace the new paradigm, until we have let go of the old. You cannot be half-hearted, making the change bit by bit. According to Thomas Kuhn, "Like the gestalt switch, it must occur all at once." The new paradigm is not figured out, but suddenly seen, it is not something we necessarily understand, but something we get.

Most times, new paradigms are received with coolness, even mockery and hostility. Paradigm pioneers are attacked for their heresy, sometimes even blasphemy. Consider, for example, Copernicus, Jesus, Martin Luther King Jr., and Gandhi. They were all persecuted even by the very people they were helping. The new idea may appear fuzzy, even bizarre, at first, because the discoverer may have made an intuitive leap and may not have all the pieces in place as yet.

Changing our paradigm means we will be asking different questions. For example we argue about the best method of teaching the curriculum of public schools, yet rarely question whether the curriculum itself is appropriate.

This ability to shift paradigms may be the most important phenomenon for the planet in the twenty-first century. We have exhausted all the options in the present paradigm and it has failed to produce any substantial change in our lives.

The potential for rescue at this time of crisis is not luck, coincidence, nor wishful thinking. Armed with a more sophisticated understanding of how change occurs, we know that the very forces that have brought us to racial and global suicide carry in them the seed of renewal. The current disequilibrium — personal, political and social — foreshadows a new kind of society. Roles, relationships, institutions, and old ideas are being reexamined, reformulated and redesigned in bold new ways — with new inspiration and hope.

We now have the control panel of change: an understanding of how transformation occurs. We are living in, the time in which we can intentionally align ourselves with nature, for the rapid remaking of our collapsing institutions and ourselves.

The affirmative and interdependent paradigm sees humanity embedded in nature. It promotes the autonomous individual in a powerful interdependent community. It sees us as stewards of all our resources, internal and external. It says that we are not victims, pawns, or limited by condition, or history. Instead we are heirs to evolutionary riches, we are capable of imagination, invention, and experiences we have only glimpsed.

The concept of a paradigm shift is especially important for all of us, because whether it is in business, education, politics or our personal lives, a paradigm change, by definition, alters the basic rules of the game. When the rules change, the entire game changes, and everyone and everything is at zero.

The Future

Most people have major insecurities about the future. For many, it is a place that is always robbing them of their security, breaking promises, changing the rules on them, causing all sorts of troubles and trials. Ironically, our greatest leverage is in the future. We cannot change the past, although if we are wise we can learn from it. Life occurs only in one place and time — here and now — the present, and we react to those events. The space of time in the present, is too slim to allow for much more. It is in the yet-to-be, the future, and only there, where we have the time to prepare for the present. If we learn to anticipate and plan for the future better, we need not fear it. In fact, we can welcome it, prepare for its coming, because more of it will be the direct outgrowth of our own efforts, ideas and visions.

By understanding and using the principle of paradigms, we will be able to anticipate and prepare in a very effective way for the future. In fact, the only way we can actually begin to change our own lives, is by recognizing the paradigm that we are functioning in, and shift to another, if the one we are in is not empowering us. By understanding the paradigm principle you will be able to open doors to your future, which would have otherwise stayed locked up, until it would have been too late.

Paradigms are like water to a fish. A fish does not know that it is in water. A fish only becomes aware of water when it is taken out of it. This is the way paradigms are to most of us, they are invisible in many situations, because it is "just the way things are." Most of the time they operate at a subconscious level, yet, they determine to a large extent, our behavior. Paradigms have a profound effect on how we live our lives, how we value those things in our lives and how we solve the problems in our lives. They are the foundation of who we are and where we are going. To ignore the power of paradigms, which influence our judgment, is to put us at significant risk when exploring the future. To be able to shape our future, we must be ready and willing to shift our paradigms.

Paradigm Opportunity

The paradigm principle offers us an opportunity to see the world in a new light and with a new vision. It provides us with a mechanism for solving old unsolvable problems, as well as new problems. The paradigm principle offers us clear directives so that we can become better strategic explorers. Our single most important skill as strategic explorers is to understand how our visions are shaped, and what influences our perception. Without that understanding, all the other skills will be only minimally useful.

In this time of crisis, we must start demanding and expecting great changes. We must start looking for new paradigms which will resolve the crisis we now find ourselves in. We have nothing to lose and everything to gain from a shift.

Moreover, all the old attempts to bring about quality of life have failed. To accept fundamentally new approaches in solving the crisis increases the opportunity to change paradigms.

Not every paradigm suggested should or will be accepted. All will have to pass the reality test and prove themselves useful over time. Many will be unsuccessful paradigms. But, if we diligently search for new and effective paradigms, we will find them. Our challenge as strategic explorers, whether our role is that of parent, entrepreneur, manager, politician, educator, citizen, or activist — is to make it easier for the new paradigms to get a fair hearing and to help the paradigm shifters feel safer. Whatever our area of endeavor, it is our responsibility to find new ways of seeing, thinking and solving our problems.

A New Paradigm of Peace, Love and Prosperity

I have a vision of a world where everyone is loved, everyone is at peace and everyone is prosperous. This vision calls for a new paradigm – a paradigm in which all of us are loving and loved, and whatever affects one of us affects all of us. This vision calls for a paradigm of abundance – where we see an infinite supply of everything we need, not only for ourselves but also for everyone on the planet. This vision also calls for each of us to be peaceful both internally and externally.

For this new paradigm to be achieved, it calls for all of us who can hold this energy to live our lives with authentic power. The earth is getting ready to shift into the next dimension and we need to shift along with it.

CHAPTER 5

INTEGRITY

A life of integrity is the only life worth living.

There is no concept as illusive as integrity — yet there is none as important and as fundamental to ones journey towards authentic power. The quality of all our human relationships whether personal, social, business or political, hinges on integrity. In fact, individuals, families, organizations and countries develop cultures of either high or low integrity.

Let's take for example a family. If parents do not practice and teach moral principles, as well as strategic values which guide the family, then it will be almost impossible for the children to learn and develop these skills. Likewise in an organization, if the leadership does not practice high integrity, then it is very likely that the rest of the organization will also follow suit.

Integrity is often confused with honesty. Honesty, frankness, openness, and truthfulness are certainly dimensions of integrity, but these are its expressions rather than its definition. Integrity is derived from the root word *integer* meaning whole or complete in and of itself. Hence integrity means to operate from the whole, to reflect the complete or totality. This means incorporating the full range of human skills — listening, thinking, reflecting, learning, questioning and intuiting. It is uprightness, righteousness, the unshakability of character, and the power to do the right thing no matter what. It is uncompromising on principles, no matter how seductive or tempting the situation may appear at the moment.

Integrity involves more than just having the right set of values; it includes having the strength of will to live with or live up to those values. Sometimes our problems are not in knowing what to do in a given situation. More often our struggle is in doing that which we know we should do. It is not simply a question of knowledge; it is equally a question of courage and determination to act consciously and righteously.

Consciousness and Integrity

Living a life of integrity is a conscious choice. Acting consciously and righteously means aligning our actions, commitments, goals, thinking and our choices with truth and principles. Living a life of integrity means paying attention to our every behavior, thought and action. It means that we cannot rely on custom, history, or tradition to carry us through. Integrity means standing on our own feet and choosing the right path.

Self-awareness is the accurate assessment of our personal integrity. It is about paying attention to our every thought, feeling and action and making sure that they align with our purpose, values, commitment and even more importantly truth principles, such as love, acceptance and compassion. It is the ability to make every moment count and to live every moment deliberately, consciously and conscientiously.

Taking a Stand

Living a life of integrity means being able to take a stand based on our values and principles. Yet most of us find it very difficult to take a stand. Why is it so difficult for us to stand up for what we believe? And to put what we believe into practice? At least four reasons come to mind.

First, we want to be liked and accepted by others. We want the affirmation and praise of others. One way to gain this acceptance is to agree with everyone else around us, or to agree with those whom we want to like and accept us. We give up our individuality, personal power, integrity and authenticity to conform to society or to others' perceptions.

Second, we try to avoid conflict and disagreement. We believe that conflict says something is wrong with a relationship. We are pulled by our desire not to upset others, so we surrender our convictions to avoid conflicts. Conflicts can be a sign that something is right, rather than wrong. It may say that you trust your friend enough to reveal your true beliefs, or that you are willing to stand up for your convictions no matter what. All great men and women of history were people who refused to surrender their integrity, who did not give in to conflict.

Third, we try to find an easy way out. Most of us are lazy, lack discipline, tenacity, courage and determination. We run from that which we know we ought to do. We try to find an easy way out of situations and circumstances. We surrender our integrity, because of this lack of discipline. The unfortunate thing is there is no easy way out. If we want to live a successful life and a life of integrity, then we must take the "bull by the horn", and accept all challenges that come our way, without running from them.

Fourth, we are all members of a tribe or society and our tribe inculcates its own attitude about integrity into us. Tribal inculcation is the most difficult challenge towards being a person of integrity. This is so, because tribal inculcation occurs at the subconscious level. We can therefore live our entire life with low integrity and not even be aware of it. To overcome this hurdle we must become aware of our culture and the ways in which it does and does not support our growth.

PERSONAL INTEGRITY ACCOUNT

We each have what we may call a "personal integrity account". This account reflects the amount of integrity and trust we have in ourselves. When we make and keep promises and commitments, such as setting and achieving goals, we make a deposit in our personal integrity account. We increase our personal power and confidence in our own trustworthiness, and in our ability to make and keep commitments to ourselves and to others. A high balance in this account, is a great source of personal power, strength and security.

When we don't achieve our goals, however, or keep our promises to ourselves and to others, we make withdrawals, and this diminishes our personal power and can become a source of great pain. Over time, frequent withdrawals cause us to lose confidence in our ability to make and keep commitments. Cynicism, doubt and rationalization follow, and these attributes sever us from the power of setting and achieving goals. Then, when we need our power and strength of character to meet critical challenges in our lives, we find that it just isn't there. When we set out to achieve something and accomplish it, such as gaining a degree, something else gets added on to us, more than that which was accomplished. This intangible thing gives us confidence and power to accomplish even more.

Building strength of character is like building physical strength. It is the same way a body builder has to go to the gym on a daily basis and work to build his muscles — we have to work on a daily basis in building our character. When the test comes, if you don't have it, no cosmetics can disguise the fact that it just isn't there. You simply cannot fake it.

It takes strength to set a heroic goal, to work on chronic problems rather than going for the "quick fix" and to stay with your commitments even when the going gets tough and the tide of popular opinion turns against you. In our Western society, we are all caught up with this quick fix mentality and instant gratification. We are sometimes prepared to sell our souls to get the quick quasi-solutions to our problems, instead of going to the integral root and paying the price for success and prosperity.

There are two human endowments that are essential for integrity; they are conscience and self-empowerment. These endowments are often misunderstood or neglected. Conscience is the moral sense of right and wrong. It is the deep connection of goals to mission, needs and principles.

Conscience is fundamental and powerful because it creates alignment between mission and principles and gives guidance in the "moment of choice". Every moment is a chance to make a choice or a decision. Every moment is an opportunity to set a goal or make a plan. Every moment in which we consciously decide to focus our time and energy towards a particular purpose is a moment of choice used consciously. What determines that choice? Is it the social mirror, the agendas of others, values that are truncated from our programs and history, needs, and capacities? Or is it a deep love-based, service-oriented, principle-centered, conscience connected and contribution focused fire within?

Goals and decisions that are connected to our inner life have the power of passion and principle. They are based on the fire within and based on fundamental principles that create quality of life results. They are founded in our purpose in life and in alignment with our personal power.

Our integrity and trustworthiness are only as high as the balance in our Personal Integrity Account. Because our integrity is the basis of our confidence in ourselves and the confidence we inspire in others, one of the greatest manifestations is the exercise of care and wisdom in building a high positive balance in our trust account.

Integrity is workability. Nothing works without integrity — it is that fundamental to every aspect of our lives — be it private or public. If there is an area in your life where you are living without integrity it just will not work. If you have a relationship in your life that you want to work – you have to make sure that integrity is the foundation on which it is built.

Building a relationship on anything but integrity is like building your house on sand. When the test comes it will simply be destroyed.

When you are out of integrity in one area of your life it affects the whole, because, integrity means wholeness. "The chain is only as strong as its weakest link." It comes down to: you are either a person of integrity or you are not. "The parts affect the whole."

THE PRICE OF INTEGRITY

Integrity is not an easy trait to have. One must be willing to pay the price for it. The price for integrity is oftentimes one's life itself. Sometimes it is not that serious. But if you have nothing for which you would die then you are not a person of integrity. A person of integrity will live up to his principles in the face of great adversity and public ridicule.

What is required is not to go with the flow but to make a difference. Deep down inside us we know this. But we too often have no backbone, no personal power or integrity to be a maverick and rock the boat. We fall to temptation and sell out on our purpose. By so doing we not only set back our own evolution but the entire evolution of mankind, because we fail to carry out our side of the bargain.

If I want to live a life of integrity I have to ask myself the following question: "Am I going to live my life's purpose and make a difference in the world, or am I going to be caught up in the rat race, trying to live in the biggest house and drive the fastest car on the block?" Too often I hear the tired phase, "I just want to be happy"; well true happiness only comes when we are living our life's purpose. Everything else is a waste of time.

Integrity occurs when our lives are integrated. When we are true to our inner calling and to higher ideals. When we keep our word and our promises consistently. When we harmonize our habits with our values and principles. Our honor becomes greater than our moods, and we can have trust and confidence in ourselves because we know ourselves. We know that we can be true and faithful under all conditions. Integrity is the foundation for true goodness, greatness and achievement. Integrity eliminates the need to show off, to exaggerate, or to boast. A life of integrity is the only life worth living.

CHAPTER 6

RESPONSIBILITY

*As long as you remain a victim you
give up your power to change.*

Responsibility simply means response-able or the ability to make a response to stimulus. That is the ability to make a conscious response to any given situation. This may sound simple enough, but it is a challenge for most of us for two major reasons. First, most of us are not conscious and therefore cannot make conscious responses. Second, some people see themselves as victims and therefore always make responses congruent with that paradigm.

We are conditioned to respond to particular stimulus in particular ways, similar to Pavlov's experiments with dogs. Ivan Pavlov (1849 – 1936) was a Russian researcher who received the Nobel Prize in physiology or medicine in 1904. He experimented with dogs, giving them signals and food, and discovered that unconditioned responses can be triggered by stimuli. This is a reactive life in which responses are a reaction to the stimulus without engaging our conscious mind. All animals are reactive, even the most intelligent. They are programmed by instinct and/or training. Some, like guard dogs, can even be trained to be responsible, but they can't take responsibility for their training. They cannot alter the programming or the instinct; in fact, they are not even aware of it. Likewise, when we are not aware of our programming we behave in a similar fashion. We react to situations and circumstances in our life out of old habits, instincts and tribal programming.

REACTIVE MODEL
Stimulus   Reaction
                Inaction

HUMAN CAPACITY

The fundamental distinguishing principle of what it is to be human is the gap between stimulus and response. That gap provides human beings with a faculty that no other animal has. That is the ability or the freedom to choose one's response. Within this gap we can exercise our human ability to be self-aware, to be imaginative, conscientious and willful. We can use these faculties to write new programs for ourselves and to choose differently from our inculcation and habits.

THE PROACTIVE MODEL

Stimulus   **Gap**   Response
             Consciousness
             Imagination
             Conscience
             Will
             Power to choose

Proactive living is the ability to create a gap between stimulus and response. This gap provides the freedom to choose and is a fundamental distinguishing characteristic of being human. There are five capabilities, namely: awareness/consciousness; imagination; conscience; independent will and the power to make choices.

Being proactive means more than taking initiative. It means that as human beings we are responsible for our own lives. Our behaviour is not just a function of our conditioning.

When we subordinate our feelings to principles, values and commitments we have the responsibility to make this happen.

If our lives appear to be out of control and a function of circumstances, it is because we have either consciously or subconsciously chosen to empower those things to control us. In giving up our power we become reactive and a victim. Conditions and circumstances affect victims. If conditions are good victims act good, if conditions are bad victims act bad. Feelings, conditions, situations and environment drive victims. As long as you remain a victim you give up your power to change. Victim relates completely in the reactive model, in which there is no gap. All of their lives is simply reactions to stimuli – little or no better than the dogs in Pavlov's experiment.

Proactive people are victors – conditions and circumstances do not affect them. Victors are proactive and have the ability to subordinate their feelings to principles, values and commitments. In life stuff happens – it is not what happens but our response to it that matters.

The starting point of personal liberation and empowerment is for you to accept total and complete responsibility for your physical, mental, emotional and spiritual well being. You are one hundred percent responsible for everything you are and for everything that you become. This is the key to authentic power, personal growth, empowerment, liberation, happiness and high achievement. You must accept that you are where you are and what you are because of yourself. If you want your situations and circumstances to change then you must change first. Your thinking determines your attitude, your conduct and your behaviour, and they in turn largely determine your success or failure in life. Because you are always free to choose the content of your conscious mind, you are always fully responsible for the consequences of what you think.

You can dream lofty dreams, learn to control your conscious and subconscious mind, attain great intellectual achievement and improve both your self-concept and self-image — but until you embrace personal responsibility — none of these efforts will bring lasting peace and success. Only by embracing one hundred percent responsibility will you mature into the wholesome and authentically powerful person you came here to be. Only through total responsibility can you achieve your full human potential.

Parental Responsibility

When you were a child, your parents were responsible for you physically, mentally, emotionally and spiritually. If you were fortunate, your parents provided you with everything. They provided you with food, shelter, clothing, education, money and whatever else you needed. Your entire needs were taken care of to some extent. You were a passive player in the process.

It is natural to be provided for by your parents during your formative years. The problems begin when people come into adulthood with the subconscious expectation that somewhere, somehow, someone else is still responsible for them and for their situation. From the age of eighteen onwards you are responsible for what you make of your life. You are the architect and builder of your destiny. Whether or not your parents succeeded in helping you to be a mature, functional, independent and self-reliant individual, from that moment forward there is no looking back. Everything you are and what you become is up to you.

No Excuses

Most of us have some excuses that we use to avoid setting clear goals and making total commitments to the things we really want. Since the quality of your thinking determines the quality of your life, you need to become a skilled thinker if you sincerely desire to fulfill your potential. Part of being a skilled thinker means that you have to examine any and all mental and emotional blocks that you may be using as an excuse for not moving ahead.

Some of the most popular excuses that people use are limiting beliefs such as "I am black", "I am white", "I am too young", "I am too old", "I am not pretty", "My parents are poor", "I am too poor" or "I can't because….".

Taking one hundred percent responsibility means no excuses. You have to come to the point in life when you decide that no matter what happens you will take total and complete responsibility and make no excuses.

No Blame

We also blame people for our plight. Total responsibility means no blame. Wherever we find ourselves we are responsible. Whining and complaining are systems of the reactive and victim personality. By blaming someone else I am saying that I am not responsible; I make myself a powerless victim; I immobilise myself in a negative situation. I also diminish my ability to influence the situation. My ability to positively influence the situation withers and dies.

The Solution

The acceptance of complete responsibility, the giving up of all your excuses, is not easy. It is one of the hardest things you will ever attempt. That is why most people never do it. This idea is a dramatic paradigm shift for many people. It is so much easier to blame other people, conditions and circumstances for our stagnant situation. However, we are responsible to control our lives and powerfully influence our circumstances.

Nelson Mandela provides a good example of proactive/victor living. Mandela was imprisoned in a South African prison for twenty-seven years, where he experienced all types of degrading and inhumane chastisement and humiliation.

Importantly however, Mandela did not tarry in self pity or blame. Instead he dwelled in the last of human freedoms — the freedom his Apartheid captors could not take away from him – the freedom to choose his own way. They could control his entire environment, they could do what they wanted with his body, but Mandela was a self-aware being who could look as an observer at his involvement. His basic identity was intact. He could decide within himself how all of this was going to affect him. Between what happened to him, or the stimulus, and his response to it, was his freedom or power to choose a response.

In the midst of his experience Mandela used his mind and his imagination to simulate real life situations. He saw himself as a free man leading a liberated and united South Africa. Though a series of such discipline – mental, emotional and spiritual, principally using memory and imagination, he exercised his small freedom until it grew larger and larger. Until he had more freedom than his Apartheid captors did.

They had more liberty and more options to choose from in their environment; but he had more freedom, more internal power to exercise his options. He became an inspiration not only to those around him, but to a whole nation and indeed to many people around the world. He helped the entire nation find meaning and dignity in their suffering and humiliation.

In the midst of the most degrading circumstances imaginable, Mandela utilizes his human capabilities of self-awareness, imagination and will power to create a gap between the stimulus and his response – demonstrating the freedom to choose his response.

Victors, proactive and powerful people are like that. They do not blame conditions, circumstances or situations for their behaviour. Their behaviour is a product of their own conscious choice, based on principles, values and commitments, rather than a product of their conditions, based on their wants, needs and feelings.

Responsibility also means making and keeping commitments to others and ourselves. Our integrity to commitments that we make is the clearest test of our proactivity and responsibility. When we make and keep commitments, even small commitments, we begin to establish an inner integrity that gives us the awareness of self-control and the courage and strength to accept more of the responsibility for our own lives. By practising responsibility in our lives our honour becomes greater than our moods, wants, needs and feelings.

CHAPTER 7

CHALLENGES

*As long as you are a victim you have
given up your power to change.*

Have you ever noticed how frazzled you get when you are faced with problems? Often repeating words to yourself such as "This should not be." "Why me?" "Oh no — not again." This is the victim's approach to dealing with problems. If we respond to the challenges in our lives from the perspective of a victim we will feel controlled, oppressed, powerless and exploited.

When you see yourself as a victim, you become reactive in life. A reactive person uses language such as "Let's fight against that, there is nothing I can do; he makes me so mad; they will not allow that; I have to do that; I can't do that; I must; if only." This perspective gives your power, responsibility and accountability away, putting others and circumstances in control. In time they decide how your life will be. Without power, responsibility and accountability for your life, you are without the resources necessary to live your full potential and you will be totally inept and incapable of solving life's challenges.

Our choices of words are of utmost importance. Your language influences your mood, behavior and action. A victim will continually use negative and reactive words and phrases to describe his or her life. When we use negative and reactive words and phrases not only are we describing our reality, but also more importantly, we are programming our subconscious mind to produce the negative results we describe. Likewise when we use positive and proactive language – we not only describe our circumstances but we are in the process programming our subconscious mind positively. We actually have a choice in the matter. For every situation we can either choose to use reactive language or we can choose to use proactive language. Let's look at some examples.

Reactive language	Proactive Language
There is nothing I can do	I have alternatives
That's just the way I am	I can choose differently
He makes me so mad	I can control my own feelings
They won't allow that	I can do it
I have to do that	I can choose appropriately
I will try	I will do it
I can't	I choose
I must	I prefer
If only	I will

Reactive language comes from a paradigm of pre-determinism. That is transferring responsibility from yourself to some other force or circumstance. "I am not response-able", that is, I am not able to choose an appropriate response. The irony with reactive language is that it becomes a self-fulfilling prophecy. You become reinforced in the paradigm that you are pre-determined, and produce evidence to support that belief. You feel increasingly victimized and out of control; not in charge of your life or your destiny. You blame outside forces — other people, circumstances, and even the stars — for your own situation.

Some people perceive problems and challenges as a nuisance, a thing to be avoided at any and all cost. That's a disempowering behavior or belief, because challenges can be truly empowering, holding wonderful hidden possibilities for change and transformation. Once you have discovered that *secret*, you begin to face each challenge or change with joy. We can change the way we see problems. Rather than something to be feared and to run away from, we can see problems as challenges and an exciting *opportunity* to grow and renew. Imagine seeing every challenge as an opportunity. This is the victor's approach to dealing with life.

When you see yourself as the victor, you become proactive in life. You become an active participant in life, instead of a spectator. When faced with a problem, a victor welcomes it, knowing that when tackled with calm, clarity and power, it will leave him or her better off than before, feeling free, self-sufficient and powerful. Power and powerful language is the ability to shape your own thoughts, feelings and behavior, thus producing the results you desire. A victor uses language such as "let's look at the alternatives, I can choose a different approach, I can control my feelings, I can create an effective presence, I will be responsible and accountable for my actions and behavior."

It is a choice we make to be victims or victors. We may make the choice unconsciously, but it is a choice we make nonetheless. Every situation that we find ourselves in we can either choose to respond from the perspective of a victor rather than a victim. Some examples are:

Victim	**Victor**
React	Act or respond
Controlled	Control
Oppressed	Free
Exploited	Self-sufficient
Respond	Choose
Powerless	Powerful
Problems	Challenges

When we see our problems as challenges, they give us the energy and confidence to tackle them and find creative ways to solve them. Challenges are the catalyst to success. The first thing we need to understand is that a challenge is not the truth. "Challenge" virtually, means false accusation. If we trace the word back through the Middle English word *calenge* and Old French word *chalenge*, all the way to the Latin word *calumniari* — and they all turn out to mean, "accuse falsely." So the only power any challenge has over you is the one *you* give it.

The most important thing about victimization is that when you see yourself as a victim, you begin to play the part. Have you ever wondered why some people seem to always end up on the victim side of all equations? That's because they want to be there. And this is the "con game" because they go around complaining that they are victims, but in actuality they do want to be victims. The victimization game can only be played when there is someone willing to play the role of a victim.

Most of us have some areas in our life where we are not taking total responsibility. We are relating as victims. Also whenever we have circumstances, which affect us negatively, and we cannot release and forgive, then we are relating as victims. For example, if a person was hurt or abused by their parents — that person can choose to live a victim's life and blame his or her parents for a lousy life. On the other hand, that person can choose to forgive his or her parents and move on to live a victor's life of responsibility and accountability.

THE VICTIM'S GAME

The victim's game is something we are being, doing or having that we are complaining and protesting about, and it is persisting. This is a kind of con game because the very things that we are complaining about we are responsible for keeping in our lives. In addition we either consciously or subconsciously derive some benefits from having these things persisting in our lives. We con other people and ourselves into believing that we are poor, helpless and powerless beings — when in fact we are powerful beyond measure.

There is always a benefit to playing the victim's game, because if they were not getting something from it, people would not be playing it. Most of us exhaust a considerable amount of time and energy complaining about things in our life. These complaints seem at times to totally control and manipulate our lives. However a closer analysis will reveal a "con game" going on, because there is always a payoff — there is something that we get from complaining. For example, having a reason to be a victim gives us a good excuse for not overcoming our obstacles; we get sympathy, pity and empathy from others; we also get to be right while we make others wrong. These are all benefits from playing the victim's game. And we all play it at some times in our life, for one reason or another.

The major problem with the victim's game is that not only is there a pay-off, but there is also an inevitable cost, which significantly outweighs the pay-off. The point is that we cannot push and pull at the same time. We have to choose to do one or the other. Likewise we cannot be successful and unsuccessful at the same time. We have to choose. If I choose success, then I have to give up all the benefits that comes with defeat. If I choose to be unsuccessful, then I have to give up all the benefits of being successful.

Benefit of being a victim	**Cost of being a victim**
Pity	Success
Good excuse	Life, Joy
Laying blame	Love/prosperity
Sympathy	Self-fulfillment
Whine and complain	Self-actualization
Be Right	Relationships

Make others wrong	Happiness
No responsibility	Self-expression
Justify	Energy/vitality
Manipulate others	Control/power
Dominate	Relationship

Many people continually complain about negative situations in their lives and how it stops them from achieving success and happiness. In affirming negative situations, your lives will become a living testament to negative results. As the old phrase goes "there is no such thing as something for nothing," so if we are getting a benefit, then there is also a price that we must pay for it. Some costs that we pay to be victims are: joy, love, peace, success, prosperity, self-fulfillment, self-actualization, happiness, self-expression, energy, vitality and great relationships. In other words, we are paying with our lives when we play the victim's game.

You must understand that as long as you continue to see yourself as a victim you have given up your power to change. You cannot want success, power, prosperity, love and joy and at the same time, hang on to your victim mentality. You have to choose, it is one or the other, because you cannot have them both. What do you want? Do you want your life to work despite the rest of the world, or would you like to have someone else to blame if you screw up? It is your decision. Only you can choose. I am reminded of an experience a few years ago at one of my seminars in Detroit. A couple who had attended a previous seminar, brought their teenage daughter to this course. I could sense the love and pain they were all experiencing. From the very beginning it was very clear to everyone present just how resentful, self-destructive and victim-oriented this young woman felt. About half way into the course, she shared with us some of her life's perils, which included two pregnancies as a teenager, drug and alcohol abuse and two prison terms. Several weeks after the seminar, I received a message from her parents; they were excited and anxiously wanted to speak with me. I agreed to meet with them for lunch when I was in Detroit the next week.

When I met them at lunch, I could hardly recognize the daughter. At lunch she spoke excitedly about the insights she received from the seminar. She explained that she realized that all her self-destructive actions stemmed from her resentfulness towards her parents; that once she realized that she was responsible and accountable for her life, she could no longer play the role of a victim — there was no one to blame, but herself. This young woman took that insight and totally transformed her life, to the point where she was unrecognizable.

We may not be able to see how we play the victim's game in our own lives — but to some extent we all play this victim's game. We play it with our spouses, our children, our parents, our employers, our employees and especially with ourselves. Each time we play the victim's game, we hand over the power and control of our lives to someone or something else.

In my early days as an attorney, I practiced criminal law almost exclusively and one of the things that struck me the most, was the relatively minute number of criminals who were prepared to take personal responsibility for their crimes. Believe it or not, our prisons are filled with people playing the victim's game. The road to recovery and rehabilitation does not and cannot begin until these men and women are ready to assume personal and total responsibility for their crimes and their lives. Anytime you find yourself blaming someone else for your fate, you are playing the victim's game and giving away your power to change that circumstance.

BECOME CONSCIOUS OF HOW YOU PLAY THE VICTIM'S GAME

The first step to overcoming our victim paradigm is to become conscious of the fact that we are playing a game. When we are able to see how we play the victim's game, we are then ready to change. Many of us continue playing this game for our entire lives without conscious awareness of what we are actually doing. You need to become conscious of the benefits that you are deriving from being a victim. Look at all your persisting complaints, whether they are about your parents, spouse, children, friends, the police, your community, other communities, your nation, other nations, your race or other races and ask yourself "What benefit am I deriving from this complaint?" Look deeply at your motive. You may be surprised to discover that you have subconsciously been seeking pity, sympathy and approval.

Once you have the consciousness of playing the victim's game and the benefits you derive from playing it, you then need to become conscious of what it is costing you. To get something, you have to give up something. For example, if I choose to believe and to complain that my life is lousy because my parents did not love me – I will consciously or unconsciously create a lousy life as evidence of my belief and complaint.

Once you are clear about the benefit and the cost, you then need to decide whether or not you still want to pay that price for those benefits. If the answer is yes, then you continue to evolve subconsciously. If the answer is no, then you have to choose to evolve consciously and to make conscious choices about the rest of your life. You will decide that the benefits you derive from playing the victim's game, are no longer desirous and you can then release that part of you which needed those benefits. You will step into the new world of consciousness, the unknown, freedom, human closeness, possibilities, responsibility and wholeness.

Face Your Problems

Wouldn't it be amazing, if we all had the guts to stand up and face our problems and challenges as they arise? If we did that we would find that we would have very little problems of any significance. Most problems when they first occur are very simple challenges that help us to grow. If we have any courage we would walk through them, learn the lesson and move on. However, because we fear every little problem which arises we often get frazzled and run, blindly believing that if we ignore our problems long enough they will go away.

Problems however, do not go away when we ignore them – they only multiply. For example, if you have a problem and you fail, refuse and/or decline to deal with it, that same problem will reappear sometime in your future, multiplied by a factor of ten. If you again fail and or refuse to deal with it, it will again reappear this time multiplied by a factor of one hundred.

Facing each problem or challenge, with integrity, grace and courage is one of the keys to living a prosperous, successful, joyous and peaceful life. Accepting our problems as challenges and taking responsibility and accountability for our lives, are some of the essential steps towards self-empowerment!

CHAPTER 8

DISCIPLINE

*Discipline is the rock on which
we must build our lives.*

Discipline is undoubtedly the single most important ingredient that I have encountered in my study of human development. It is the driving force on the pathway toward human success.

Some of us equate discipline with coercion. That is, we think of discipline as someone with power and/or authority imposing his or her will, on his or her subordinates. When we relate to discipline in a coercive manner, we invariably miss the tremendous power and life enhancing richness that discipline has to offer.

In fact, one of the main reasons for our decrepit state is the lack of self-discipline. This is true for our physical, mental, emotional, and spiritual health as well as our economic and social states. For example, if we are physically fit and in good health, this is directly related to the amount of discipline we exercise toward our physical body, such as eating in the appropriate manner and exercising appropriately.

As any coach or teacher will tell you, a disciplined student will ultimately perform much better than an indisciplined student with greater ability and aptitude. This holds true for adults as well. The adults that succeed are those that have learned to discipline their minds; consequently, they usually read more, attend self-development courses and work on bettering themselves and enhancing their careers.

Economic prosperity is one of the areas in which discipline will make the most profound difference. Many persons will argue that our impoverishment should be blamed on someone else, or on some particular set of circumstances or situations. Do not believe them. Any set of circumstances can be overcome if we are disciplined enough to seek and find the right answers to our problems.

In fact, most of us silently or publicly wish that we could live our lives without problems, not understanding those problems can be blessings in disguise. We cry incessantly about the multitude of our problems. We seem to believe that life should be generally easy.

Most of us believe that our difficulties represent a unique kind of affliction. We believe that somehow these problems have been especially visited upon us and not upon others. I know about this kind of moaning, because I have done my fair share of it.

If we would come to the realization and acceptance of the fact that life is difficult and that there are problems, we would be in a position to apply the requisite amount of discipline to lead a healthy, successful and prosperous life. There is no way of living a successful life without facing our problems.

I like what Dr. Scott Peck said in his book *"The Road Less Traveled"* — he states:

> "Life is difficult. This is a great truth. It is a great truth because once we truly see this truth, we transcend it. Once we truly know that life is difficult — once we truly understand and accept it — then life is no longer difficult. Because once it is accepted, the fact that life is difficult no longer matters."

Discipline is the fundamental ingredient that will help us to solve the problems we experience. With total discipline we will solve all of our problems, with some discipline, we will solve some of our problems, and with no discipline we will not solve any of our problems.

I can now imagine a parent reading this chapter and as a result start coercing his or her children. Let me remind you that discipline and coercion are two different things. Old child rearing philosophies adhere to the old saying "don't spare the rod and spoil the child." We have taken this to mean that we should spank our children to ensure that they obey our instructions and become "disciplined". Not so! We teach only fear by using coercion. The best way to teach discipline to our children is to love them and set the example for them to follow.

The old saying "who you are speaks so loudly I cannot hear what you are saying", is absolutely true here. For example, if a father routinely watches television for 2 to 3 hours every night, while forcing his children to study, it just will not work. The point is, if a parent wants to have disciplined children, the parent must first be disciplined.

Let's move this concept of discipline to another level. I believe that getting on a spiritual path requires firm commitment and discipline to having congruency and harmony between our thoughts, our feelings and our behavior. All higher spiritual paths with which I am familiar, emphasize both physical and mental discipline as an essential prerequisite to spiritual growth and development.

Essential to discipline is the notion of sacrifice. We must recognize that there is a price to be paid for everything in our life — be it desirable or undesirable. If we want desirable things then we must be prepared to delay gratification and make certain sacrifices to obtain them.

Discipline and Personal Power

In every realm of life, whether social, political, national or individual, the race belongs to the disciplined. However, there is no place where discipline is as evident as in one's personal power. In the battle of ideas the disciplined mind has the advantage over the scatterbrain. A trained mind can evaluate evidence, think logically, select ends, and devise means; it can concentrate on essentials and discard the irrelevant. A trained mind can think more rapidly and also more accurately. At the same time the man with the ready mind is more apt to express himself coherently and persuasively. Consequently the man whose mind is undisciplined will soon be outclassed and outdistanced by others in whatsoever field he enters. He will find himself not only on a lower scale socially and economically, but dominated politically by those who are more efficient.

Discipline of the body is of importance as well. It can be indispensable to authentic power if its object is to train the body to serve the mind in the attainment of worthy objectives. It makes little or no sense to have a disciplined mind on a decayed or decaying body. Therefore, discipline must be approached in a holistic manner.

A disciplined mind and a disciplined body are essential for a disciplined character. This is where most of us fail. Too many of us are weak as persons. We may have an outstandingly strong ability, which may be cultivated by intense training within a narrow sphere, such as tennis or golf, without general strength of character. But if one lacks personal power and self-discipline, his specialized ability will be progressively choked by the growth of vices until it will be lost.

You develop a disciplined character, striving to achieve balance in your life by bringing all your faculties and powers under control. You instill order, consistency, and purpose in your life. As a result you will develop poise and grace. There is no panic or self-pity. There is courage and tenacity to meet life and conquer it. There is a powerful sense of responsibility and accountability to meet ones duty.

Self-discipline is the mark of maturity. It is the ability to regulate conduct by principle and judgment rather than impulse, desire or social custom. It is the ability to subordinate appetites, wants and feelings for your commitments and your goals. It is also the ability to subordinate the body and its physical appetites to the service of the mind. For example, if you make a commitment to develop a particularly fit and attractive body – it will take self-discipline to do so.

Feelings are another important area in which we must exercise discipline. When we unconsciously follow our feelings – it can lead us into impulsive and irresponsible behavior. Most of the times we don't consciously choose our feelings and therefore we have little or no control over how we feel at a particular moment. If we continue to live as a result of our unconscious feelings we will forever be pulled and pushed by the wind and the tide. Discipline means that we develop the habit of living from our words and our commitments and not from our feelings. This could be as simple as – I may be committed to doing a certain task at work, but I honestly don't feel like doing it. Now what do I do? Do I follow my feelings or my commitment? The answer is clear and unambiguous for the disciplined person. The commitments always win out over feelings and wants.

Disciplined character also means the mastery of moods. People without authentic power are prey to their mood swings. You have seen people like that; you go into work wondering what mood they are going to be in that day. People, events, situations and circumstances can alter their moods one way or another. These people exercise little or no discipline over their moods.

We must cultivate that fixedness of purpose, that steadiness of faith, that quiet, almost rhythmic, performance of duty, which gradually chastens our moods, cleansing from them their fierce wildness and bringing them into keeping with our total pattern. Then our moods will fluctuate much less. Even if it swings, it will not swing so far. We must be conscious and pay attention to our moods so that we can alter them when needed to be in alignment with our goals, commitment and purpose.

The most critical area in which we have to exercise discipline is in our speech. Regardless of how carefully controlled a person is at all other points, no-one can qualify for the high rating of a truly disciplined character whose tongue is not restrained by prudence and directed by the rein of love. One may have a disciplined body, a disciplined mind, a disciplined will, even disciplined emotions, appetites and habits, but a loose tongue betrays a fatal fault in the armor. In fact there are some disciplined people who will not respond to another out of anger. They will wait until the anger or emotions have cooled off before giving a response. This delay helps them to respond to a stimulus rather than react to it.

Some people pride themselves on their frankness. "I say what I feel", or "I say what I think," they boast. They do not understand that discipline and integrity occurs more in our words and actions rather than in our thoughts and feelings. We have total conscious control over our words and actions but not over our thoughts and feelings. Frankness is indeed a virtue when coupled with intelligence, love, tact and discretion. But it can become a vice when it is merely the unbridled erupting of opinion without regard to time and place or human feelings. It often takes a far higher display of discipline to refrain from speaking than it does to speak.

I think that the quintessential element of discipline is keeping our word. That is making our word law. That is making and keeping promises especially to ourselves and to our loved ones. If we treat our word as law and we don't give our word unless we intend to follow through on it, life will become much more pleasurable, successful and prosperous.

Now it is okay to not give your word. So if someone wants you to commit to something that you don't want to commit to, you just don't! You remain congruent and integral. However, if you do commit to a request, then you make your word law. You do what you have committed to. So one has to be very, very careful about what one commits to.

If I say "look, I am going to lose ten pounds within the next two weeks" that's really what I am going to do. I put my word out there, then I make my conduct consistent with that proclamation and that's really the essence of discipline. That's really all it is. Discipline is one of the most powerful concepts in personal development.

PRIORITIES

Another place for us to exercise authentic power and self-discipline is in choosing priorities appropriately. Many of us spend much of our time doing things that are in no way important to our goals. We procrastinate and waste time. Prioritization is one of the most crucial problems of life. On its solution hangs success or failure, improvement or degeneration.

We must be able to choose first things first. This involves the rejection of activities that clamor for our attention, and prevents us from getting more important things done. All of us are confronted by a bewildering multiplicity of claims upon our time, talent, money, and loyalties. The claims are not only legion, but also loud and insistent. To attempt to satisfy even half of them would result in frittering life away to nothingness. If our life is to be fruitful and purposeful, we must heroically and decisively cut away many of the possible activities, which could clutter every single day of our lives.

We cannot be everything to everybody at every time.

Therefore we must select. Saying no to something gives you the opportunities of saying yes to others things that are more in alignment with your goals, purpose and commitments. Whatever one's goals may be, they can be achieved only by the sacrifice of the lesser. This requires discipline of a high order. We must put first things first, and do it no matter how much more pleasant and appealing other things may appear to be at the moment.

PART III

THE MENTAL

The Nature of the Human Mind
The Subconscious Mind
The Superconscious Mind
The Law of Thinking

CHAPTER 9

THE CONSCIOUS MIND

*We presently use less than 5% of our minds
— if we want to experience more power in
our lives — we must expand the usage of our
minds.*

Most of us confuse the human mind with the human brain. The mind is a powerful energy of the mental dimension; it is a part of the ego equipment. The mind is not part of the physical body even though it permiates every cell of the phycial body. At one stage all human being were just one cell. One half contributed by our fathers and the other half contributed by our mothers. This one cell divides and mulitply to form every cell of our bodies. The first cell contains energy and matter as we know it but it also contained something else which we can distinguish as intelligence or information. This intelligence is what we refer to as mind stuff. The entire universe is made up of just two things energy and information. These two things are present in varing degrees in everything in existence.

The brain on the other hand, is a physical organ of the physical body. The brain is a marvellously constructed bio-computer, electrochemical switchboard and calculating machine. Most of its practical use is as a large automatic control center for body functions like breathing, walking, and digesting food. The frontal part of the brain is capable of what is called conditioned reflex. This involves the forming of relations between cause and effect and forming memory responses. Scientists tell us that human beings are only using a very small portion of their brain, just about five percent.

Some scientists say that if we were able to use our mind more effectively we would present a greater level of intelligence. Greater intelligence means greater abilities and proficiency. How can we increase this mental power? How can we tap into that unused ninety five percent of our mental capacity? The brain as we know it is based on the five senses and the ability to think. This is very different from the mind, which is not mechanical at all, but rather spiritual and mystical. Mind power is one of the greatest forces available to human beings. It is one of our greatest treasures. It is like a doorway to our true home, yet no one can see it and it cannot be found. It is the source of our consciousness. It is a body of power and light. Without its power we would not be conscious. Consciousness is what distinguishes human beings from other life forms on this planet.

The mind can be divided in four main parts: Superconscious, conscious, subconscious, and unconscious. Each part is vitally important and has distinct functions. Each part has to be understood and used appropriately for us to maximize the potential of the mind.

The Three Parts of the Mind
Superconscious or Universal Mind

Inspiration,   Creativity
Serendipity,   Synchronicity
Higher Mind,
    Access to untapped information
    Solution to every problem
    Brings answers you need
Seat of the higher self and soul

Conscious Mind
Choices, Decide
I Am
Subjective consciousness
Seat of the Individual I AM

Subconscious
Huge memory bank, History, Programming, Conditioning, Inculcation, Virtually unlimited, Wants, needs
Stores all experiences, Habits, likes, feelings
Stores/retrieves data Subjective
Feelings based on history, Servant
Works constantly to bring into being your desires
Seat of the inner child and the ego

Unconscious Mind
Involuntary activities
Unconscious
Seat of the unconscious activity

THE CONSCIOUS MIND

The conscious mind seems to be the logical place to start the exploration of the human mind. As it is the single most determinative factor in what distinguishes human being from every other creature on the panet. Without the conscious mind we could not be classified as human beings at all, we may be classified as human doing, human animals but not human beings. Being implies an autonomous individual capable of choosing ones out way and of living an authentic life.

The unfortunate thing is that most of us do not use the power of our conscious mind. We relegate that power to our subconscious mind. But the subconscious mind does not really have the power to make choices, rather it simply run programs that are inculcated in it. By the time be become teenagers the subconscious mind has a programmed reaction for almost every situation. If we never wake up and learn to use our conscious minds we will live our entire life as a human computer just reacting out of our old programs.

The powers to choose, will, and decide are the earmarks of the conscious mind. Yet these attributes are most often relegated to the subconscious mind. These powers are vastly underrated by humanity. Living consciously deserves a respect and attention that can hardly be put into words. Your conscious mind is like the captain of a ship or the pilot of a plane. The captain determines where the ship will go. You can choose to ride on an ocean of opportunity and ride to harbors of prosperity, or you can misuse your consciousness and live in a swamp.

The problem is that we have let our consciousness mull in habitual negativity, self-rejection and needless limitation. When we decide to use our thinking in a new way, we will experience the truth of life's changeability; life's endless possibility to move into new directions. We can constantly expand our thinking, take in new ideas, embrace new realizations, and therefore bring to ourselves new will-directions, new expansion, new aims, new energies, and new feelings. These new ways of thinking and feeling change those attitudes we now dislike so much.

One of the most fundamental things about the conscious mind is the power to make choices. Each situation you are in contains new possibilities for reaction, response or action. You have choices all the time. You can be in a new situation and automatically fall into your old conditioned programs and reflexes, a negative approach, without paying attention to what you are doing. Many people moan and complain about the misery of life because things have happened that they do not like, and they never see the connection between their discontent and failures on the one hand, and their one-sided, negative automatic reaction on the other.

As long as you assume that this habitual approach is the only one possible, you will not grasp the possibilities and powers of your mind. Conscious choice is at the center of human evolutionary process. Each choice that we make is a choice of intention. What you choose, with each action and each thought, is an intention, a quality of consciousness that you bring to your life. We mustunderstand that whatever our results are, it is what we intended. The reason why we think that we sometimes have a different result from our intention is because we have different parts of us with different intentions that we are not conscious of. Most of us have several aspects. One aspect may be loving, charitable and trusting. Another may be fearful, vindictive and selfish. If you are not conscious of all the different parts of yourself the parts that are strongest will win out over the other parts.

To choose your intentions consciously you must become aware of the different aspects of yourself. If you are not conscious of each of the different aspects of yourself, you will have the experience of wanting to be, do, say or intend one thing, but finding yourself being, doing, saying or intending something else. You will want your life to move in one direction, and find that it is moving in another. You will desire to release a painful pattern from your experience, and see it appear yet again.

As you become conscious of the different aspects of yourself, you will be able to consciously experience the forces within you that compete for expression, that lay claim to the single intention that is yours at each moment, that will shape your destiny. When you enter these dynamics consciously, you create for yourself the ability to choose consciously among the forces within you, to choose when and how you will focus your energy. The choice not to choose is the choice to live from your subconscious and to be irresponsible. Awareness of the different aspects of your personality and of the need for wholeness and integration brings with it the need for conscious choice. Each decision requires that you choose which parts of yourself you want to cultivate, and which parts you want to replace.

A responsible choice is a choice to be aware of the consequences of each choice. In order to make responsible choices you must ask yourself before each choice you are considering; "What will this produce? Do I really want to create that? Am I ready to accept all of the consequences of this choice?" Try to see all the possible outcomes from the choice you are considering. Test the water and see how you feel. Ask yourself "Is this what I really want?" and then decide. When we choose consciously we choose responsibly. Responsible choice is taking the consequences of your choices into consideration before
you make the choice.

Responsible choice is the process by which we live from love and release the strangle hold of fear. It is the process through which we can nurture the needs of the soul and challenge and release the needs of the ego. Responsible choice is the choice of clarity, love and wisdom. It is the choice of conscious change and transformation. It is the choice of the higher frequency energy currents of love, forgiveness, compassion and integrity. It is the choice to listen and follow the wisdom of your higher self, and your soul, rather than your ego. It is the choice of authentic power, rather than superficial ego power.

When you feel unhappy or hopeless you must question yourself. Ask yourself, "Do I have another way to respond to this situation that seems to befall me out of nowhere, and to which I choose to act negatively, destructively, making myself hopeless, complaining and feeling angry about it?" The choice is yours. Your anger and complaints against the world are wasted energy. All that energy could do so much to build new life for you if it were used properly. You cannot change others, but you can use your awareness to change your own attitudes, and your thinking. Then life offers its limitless possibilities to you.

Consciousness is the ability to be aware of yourself and what you are thinking, being and doing. It is the ability to separate yourself from your body, emotions, intellect, history and experiences and to observe them, recognizing them as tools you use but not your essence. When we are not aware we get caught in a vicious circle of living out of our habits, and our history - repeating the same old scripts over and over again. Consciousness is the most important faculty of the human mind. When we use it appropriately – we can bring into our experience all that we need physically, emotionally, mentally and spiritually, to accomplish our purpose here on earth. When we don't use or misuse our consciousness our life becomes like a ship on the open sea without a captain or a navigator, no sense of direction or purpose. Wherever we end up is by pure accident. Without consciousness we often take on the characteristics of our tribe and act out of the fears of our own subconscious and the collective subconscious of the tribe.

CHAPTER 10

THE SUBCONSCIOUS MIND

*Whatever the mind conceives and
believes it will achieve.*

There is a poem written by Margaret E. White about the subconscious mind that gives a clear picture of how it works. It goes like this:

I AM VERY ACCOMMODATING

I ask no questions
I accept whatever you give me.
I do whatever I am told to do.
I do not presume to change anything you
think, say, or do;
I file it all away in perfect order, quickly
and efficiently,
and then I return it to you exactly as you
gave it to me.
Sometimes you call me your memory.
I am the reservoir into which you toss
anything your heart
or mind chooses to deposit there.
I work night and day; I never rest, and
nothing can impede my activity.
The thoughts you send to me are
categorized and filed and my filing system
never fails.

I am truly your servant who does your
bidding without hesitation or criticism.
I co-operate when you tell me that you are
"this" or "that" and I play it back as you give
it. I am most agreeable.
Since I do not think, argue, judge, analyze,
question, or make decisions,
I accept impressions easily.
I am going to ask you to sort out what you
send me,
however; my files are getting a little
cluttered and confused. I mean, please discard
those things that you do not want returned to
you.
What is my name? Oh, I thought you knew!
I am your subconscious.

Your subconscious mind can be your best friend or your worst enemy depending on how you use it. If we program our subconscious mind responsibly and appropriately we will reap the fruits of our labor. If we fail to program our subconscious mind or program it irresponsibly and inappropriately we will suffer the unpleasant results.

Your subconscious mind is like a huge memory bank. Its capacity is virtually unlimited. It permanently stores everything that ever happened to you, even before birth, until you die. Your subconscious memory is virtually flawless. It is our attempt to access this memory that is suspect. The function of your subconscious mind is to store and retrieve data. Its job is to ensure that you respond exactly the way that you are programmed. Your subconscious mind makes everything you say and do fit a pattern consistent with your self-concept, your "master program."

Your subconscious mind is subjective. It does not think

or reason independently; it merely obeys and carries out the commands it receives from your conscious mind. Your conscious mind can be thought of as a gardener, planting seeds, while your subconscious mind can be thought of as the garden, or fertile soil, in which the seeds germinate and grow.

Your conscious mind is like a master that commands and your subconscious mind is like a servant that obeys. Your subconscious mind is an unquestioning servant that works day and night to make your behavior fit a pattern consistent with your emotionalized thoughts, beliefs, hopes, desires and fears. Your subconscious mind grows either flowers or weeds in the garden of your life, whichever you plant by the mental equivalents you create. Your subconscious mind is impartial and neutral — it will bring you whatever you focus your energy on. If you focus on fear it will manifest in your life exactly what you fear. It does not pick and choose between your commands it brings exactly what you command – be it good, bad or indifferent.

Your subconscious mind has what is referred to as a homeostatic impulse. It keeps your body temperature at a constant degree. It keeps your breathing regulated and keeps your heart beating at a regular pace plus a host of other bodily functions in harmony. Your subconscious mind also practices homeostasis in your mental realm, by keeping your being, doing, thinking and acting in a manner consistent with what you have done and said in the past. Everything you have, been, done, thought, or said in the past is stored in your subconscious mind. It has memorized all your comfort zones and works to keep you in them. Your subconscious mind causes you to feel emotionally, physically and mentally uncomfortable whenever you attempt to do anything new or different, or to change any of your established patterns of behavior.

If you want to be successful you will have to consciously push yourself out of this comfort zone. You will have to stretch yourself or else your comfort zone will become a rut. Complacency is one of the greatest enemies of success, possibilities and creativity. For you to accomplish something new – something which is not yet programmed into your subconscious mind – such as learning to ride, drive or learning to play tennis – you will have to be willing to feel awkward and uncomfortable doing it the first few times. If it is worth doing, it is worth the awkwardness until it is programmed into your subconscious mind and that mind will simply take over with effortless ease.

The Law of Subconscious Activity

The nature of subconscious activity is that any idea or thought that you accept as true in your conscious mind will be accepted without question by your subconscious mind, which will then immediately start acting to bring your command into reality. Your subconscious mind is the seat of the Law of Attraction, the sending station of mental vibration and thought energy. When you begin to believe that something is possible for you, your subconscious mind begins to broadcast mental energies and you begin to attract people, situations and circumstances in harmony with your dominant thoughts.

When you begin to think about a new goal your subconscious takes this thought as a command and begins to work on it. It begins to realign your life experiences in such a way that your whole life becomes congruent with your new goals. Your words, actions and behavior will be adjusted so they are consistent with you achieving your goals. You begin to meet the right people, do the right things and say the right things to help you move towards your goals. But you must focus your conscious mind.

Methods of Programming the Subconscious Mind

Focus and Concentration

Whatever you focus and concentrate you energy on will grow. The more you think about something the more it becomes your reality. If you want to be successful you have to be able to concentrate your thought single-mindedly on one thing and to stay with it until it is realized. You have to learn to discipline yourself and to think only of what you want and not about what you don't want. This is how you have to use your conscious mind to control your subconscious mind. Because your subconscious mind brings what you focus on into reality. You therefore have to guard the doorway of your conscious mind diligently. You must dwell on your purpose and desires for the future and refuse to focus on your fears and doubts.

Law of Substitution

Since the conscious mind can only hold one thought at a time you can substitute one thought for another. This allows you to deliberately replace a negative thought with a positive thought. In so doing you take control of your subconscious programming, and your emotional life. This law is the key to happiness, to positive mental attitude and to personal liberation. It can change your life, your conversations, your emotions, your attitude and your feelings.

You can use the law of mental substitution to replace any negative or fearful thought that may be troubling you. You can deliberately substitute a positive thought in its place. When you are feeling fearful just surround yourself with love and light and think of peace, calm and tranquility. Immediately your mood and feelings will change and you will not be fearful anymore. When you feel self-pity or self-doubt, just think of your purpose, vision, mission and goals. You will feel a sense of well-being and worthiness.

One of the best ways to change your mind from negative to positive is to stop thinking about the problem and start thinking about the solution. Shift your mind from focusing on the past to focusing on the possibilities for the future.

Affirmations

Affirmations are strong statements or commands from your conscious mind to your subconscious mind. They override past negative information and replace them with new positive information and thoughts, influencing positive behavior. Affirmations must be positive, present tense and personal, such as "I love myself", "I am Prosperous", "I am successful" and "everyday in every way I am getting better and better and better". When you repeat these continually your subconscious mind accepts these as valid descriptions and brings about the reality of them.

Affirmations can change your life immeasurably. Strong affirmations repeated many times daily can bring about immediate personality changes. You can boost your courage, increase your enthusiasm, control your emotions, and build up your self-esteem by repeating statements of the person you want to be.

Affirming aloud by yourself or with others can increase the intensity of the experience and bring about a greater impact on your subconscious mind. Just stand in front of a mirror and repeat many times "I can do it", "I love myself", "you are the best". If you are on a team repeat "we are the best", "we are the champs". This will also build your self/team confidence and self-image. Anything that you say aloud with conviction and enthusiasm has more impact than something that you say in your mind. That is why it is very important to keep your conversation cheerful, optimistic and positive. You will be amazed at the significant impact this conscious choice will have on your subconscious mind and your life.

VISUALIZATION

This is one of the main ways of programming your subconscious mind. The visual images you hold in your conscious mind will be transferred to your subconscious mind and become your reality. They will deepen and intensify your desire, belief, willpower and persistence. The intensity, frequency, vividness and duration of your visualization will have a positive effect on bringing your desire into reality.

Your subconscious mind cannot tell the difference between a real experience and one that you intensely and vividly image. Every time that your conscious mind imagines, recollects, remembers or re-experiences an event, your subconscious mind accepts it and stores it exactly as if you had just actually repeated it.

One way to utilize the law of visualization is to create a personal "treasure map" of all that you want in your life. Design a poster for your wall with a picture of yourself and all the things you want your subconscious mind to bring into your life. Cut out pictures, headlines and quotations from magazines and newspapers and paste them all over this poster. Create a powerful visual representation of the ingredients that symbolize success and achievement for you.

All improvements in your life begin with an improvement in your mental image. Your mental images trigger thoughts, feelings, words and actions consistent with them. Visualization activates all the powers of the subconscious mind and brings them to work for you.

RELEASE ALL CONCERN

Once you have given a clear command to your subconscious, don't worry. Just release it and let it go. Your subconscious mind will deliver your request to your superconscious mind and it will go to work for you. Don't be attached to the result. Just release it to the esoteric powers of your mind and the universe. Then sit back and enjoy the fruits of your design.

CHAPTER 11

THE SUPERCONSCOUS MIND

*All extraordinary achievements are
based on the appropriate use of the
superconscious mind.*

The superconscious mind is the secret of the ages. It is the key to health, happiness and prosperity. When you use your superconscious mind correctly you will be able to solve any problem, overcome any obstacle and achieve any goal you sincerely desire. All personal greatness and individual achievements are based on proper use of the superconscious mind. In fact everything we have discussed up to this point has been preparing you to use this power of your superconscious mind to transform the quality of your life. Ralph Waldo Emerson said we live in the midst of an immense intelligence that responds to our every need. He compared this intelligence to an ocean and said that when we receive insights from it we will recognize them as coming from far beyond our own limited mind.

The superconscious mind is a source of inspiration for all creative beings. The superconscious mind is responsible for all new inventions and scientific breakthroughs. The superconscious mind is the source of all inspiration, all motivation and excitement that you feel when aroused by a new idea or possibility. It is the source of intuition and of flashes of insight. It is the "still small voice" within. Whenever you have been wrestling with a problem and suddenly come up with a great idea that turns out to be the perfect solution, you are tapping into your superconscious mind.

Every time you experienced a new insight into a challenge you were facing your superconscious mind was working. Your superconscious mind has access to all knowledge in your subconscious mind but more importantly it has access to knowledge beyond your subconscious mind. It can access information and knowledge from outside and beyond your personal knowledge and experience. It actually lies outside your brain, outside your conscious and your subconscious mind.

The superconscious mind is a universal mind that contains all the intelligence, ideas and knowledge that have ever existed or that will ever exist. Two people in different parts of the world can be working on a problem that has never been solved before and they can simultaneously come up with the same answer, which is the only answer available for that particular problem, at the same time with no communication, whatsoever. That is because the universal mind, the superconscious mind, operates everywhere and through everything.

Once you start using your superconscious mind you will start getting ideas and insights from out of the blue. For example, many people have an insight and they do nothing with it and then one day all of a sudden they see somebody else doing the same thing they thought of doing before. The difference between the two people is that the one who acted on the superconscious insight simply had more trust and confidence in his or her ability to turn the idea into reality. Because of our childhood conditioning we lose confidence and trust in ourselves, in our ideas, in our intuition. We don't believe that we can make a difference or that we can change the world. However, when we begin to accept and value the insight of our superconscious mind we will be amazed at the kind of ideas that come to us and the next time we have an idea we will do something with it.

Your superconscious mind functions on a non-conscious level twenty-four hours a day. Once you have programmed a goal or problem into your conscious mind and released it, it is then transferred to your subconscious mind and your superconscious mind goes to work on it. You can go on with your daily life, with your conscious and subconscious energies focused on the work at hand, while your superconscious mind is busy working on the request that you released to it.

The superconscious mind is accessed through your conscious and subconscious mind. As we have discussed before, the conscious mind identifies, compares, analyzes, decides and chooses. The subconscious mind stores and retrieves information and obeys the commands of the conscious mind. The superconscious mind functions outside and beyond both of them but is accessed through them.

Your superconscious mind responds best to clear authoritative commands or what are called positive affirmations. Every time that you affirm a goal or a desire in your conscious mind, your subconscious mind activates your superconscious mind to release the idea and energy that you need to bring your desire into reality. This is why decisiveness is such an important trait of successful men and women because they know exactly what they want. Their superconscious powers are working for them, continuously. You will also find that when you stop vacillating and make a firm clear decision that you are going to do something no matter what the cost, everything suddenly starts to work in your favor.

When you affirm "I love myself" or "I can do it" or "I make x million dollars per year" you are programming yourself in the most powerful way possible. You are turning on the master switch to all your mental powers. Your job is to keep the conscious mind focused on your thoughts, goals, purpose and mission. Your superconscious mind will automatically and continuously solve each problem on your way to your goal or mission as long as you have sent clear messages to your subconscious mind. When a problem arises you can trust absolutely in your superconscious powers to function for you as long as your goals are clear.

Your superconscious mind operates only in a mental climate of faith, acceptance, love and trust. The attitude of confidently expecting that your problems will be solved, obstacles removed and your goals achieved, is the mental state that intensifies the rate of vibration and thoughts and causes your superconscious mind to function at its best.

Your superconscious mind works best when there is detachment. You don't have to think about the outcome of any situation that you need to resolve. The outcome will always be everything that you can ask for or something better. It seems that the harder you don't try the better your superconscious mind works. You must have faith and trust the universe. You have to develop the childlike ability to entrust yourself to the goodness of the universe.

You have to develop an attitude of calmness and confidence and resist any kind of negativity. Negativity shuts down your superconscious mind and diminishes your power. Any kind of negativity, anger, sorrows or fear shuts down your superconscious mind. It clouds your thinking and confuses the messages you are sending from your conscious mind to your subconscious mind. Negative emotions of any kind interfere with the calm positive attitude your superconscious mind requires for optimum functioning.

Your superconscious mind brings you the experiences you need to grow holistically. It guides you and walks you through the obstacles, circumstances, and situations that will prepare you to achieve what you ask for. You cannot achieve anything on the outside, which is not already on the inside. The superconscious mind therefore prepares you on the inside by bringing experiences that you need to grow. When you are at a level to receive your goal, your superconscious mind will simply have it appear out of nowhere for you. So that when you actually receive your goal it seems anticlimactic, it comes to you through the steps that you have already taken in life.

This is a very important point because if you receive anything on the outside that you have not already prepared for on the inside this would be incongruent. The outer would be incongruent with the inner and the inner desires always prevail. Therefore, if you were suddenly given a gift that you were not prepared for or you won the lottery or all of a sudden you became rich but your inner consciousness is not congruent with being wealthy or rich you will do your damnedest to get rid of it. You will do your best to get rid of the riches on the outside that are not congruent with the way you are on the inside. That is why you see a lot of people who move from rags to riches very quickly move back to rags just as fast. As the saying goes; "easy come easy go".

If you achieve your success gradually on the inside, before you seek to have it manifested on the outside, not only will you achieve your goals, your vision, and purpose but you will find that you will be able to hold on to all the goodness that comes to you. You will find yourself in a prepared state of readiness to receive your rewards. If you should look back at your life you will see that the great things that you accomplished occurred when you were ready for them. Worthwhile goals are often preceded by some amount of difficulty or anxiety, sometimes even fear. But once you work through the fears and you finally accomplish the goals, they are actually anticlimactic. You know what you have done and you know that you deserved what you desired. You expected the results you got.

Our superconscious mind is like a schoolteacher and it sends lessons for us to learn so we can grow. Whenever we fail a test we have to repeat it until we get it. There is no automatic move-up — we have to learn each lesson. Our superconscious mind is also very patient; every lesson must be learned.

Your superconscious mind works with synchronicity and serendipity. Synchronicity is a phenomenon that occurs when two seemingly unrelated events happen at the same time. Both of these events help you to move towards your goals. Serendipity is the facility of making happy discoveries, not sought for. People who experience serendipity all seem to have one thing in common, they are actively seeking something. They all seem to have a very clear goal and the remarkable things that they find are associated with something they want to accomplish.

SUPER-CONSCIOUS ACTIVITY

The law of superconscious activity states that any thought, plan, goal or idea that we have in our conscious mind must be brought into reality by our subconscious and superconscious minds.

This law explains how we create our world by the thoughts that we allow to dominate our thinking. If we keep our minds on the things that we want and keep them off the things that we fear, our goals, whatever they are, will eventually materialize and become our reality. This law is mutual, it works the same way for everybody. If you use it for good then good will come into your life; if you use this for negativity it will bring illness, unhappiness and financial frustration. You are free to choose the kind of life that you live.

Our superconscious mind is the seat of our higher self and our soul. Whenever we are working on a problem which the conscious mind cannot solve, there comes a point when all we have to do is stop the conscious activity and allow superconscious activity to take over. The superconscious mind, which has all the answers to all problems, will send the answer to the conscious mind. The conscious mind will get the message at exactly the right time, therefore you must act on it immediately. If you get the urge to telephone someone or to say something or to do something and it feels exactly right, act in faith and trust and follow your instinct, it will always turn out to be the right thing to do.

FIVE STEP APPROACH TO SOLVING PROBLEMS.

1. Confusion and Definition

Define the problem that you are working on. This is sometimes the stage of confusion, because sometimes, you cannot put your finger on what the problem really is. Once you think you know what the problem is (NB: doesn't writing help you to define the problem?) write it out as best you can before moving on to the next stage. You have to stay with the problem for a little bit until you can clearly define what it is.

2. Exploration

Explore the problem — get as much information as you can read. Read, research, ask questions and actively seek the answer that you need. Explore every facet of the problem to see if you can find the solution for the problem at a conscious level (NB Why search for solutions at this level at all – why not just release everything to superconscious?).

3. Incubation

If you still have not been able to solve the problem consciously then turn it over to the superconscious mind. You simply release it, in confidence that the problem will be solved. Turn it over to your subconscious and superconscious minds. Release it confidently, the way you would release a balloon and let if float away. Get your conscious mind busy elsewhere. Don't concentrate on the problem, just release it and let it go.

4. **Illumination**
This is the stage where insight comes to you from nowhere. You just happen to have an "aha" experience. Where the answer to the problem you have been struggling with just appears to you from out of nowhere. This is how synchronicity and serendipity come into play.

5. **Celebration**
Celebrate and give thanks and express gratitude to your subconscious and superconscious minds and to your higher self, for giving you the answer that you requested.

Pure Consciousness

Consciousness, in its pure state, is absolute: More absolute than the speed of light, which slows on entering a material medium such as the earth's atmosphere; more absolute than the existence of matter, which is only a manifestation of energy; more absolute than energy, which itself is a vibration of consciousness.

Only in humankind does consciousness reveal its potential for abandoning its material identity altogether. The fact that human beings seem to possess a capacity for increasing our awareness indefinitely suggests that we may even have the potential to continue that expansion to infinity.

Actually, there is only one state of consciousness: super-consciousness. The conscious and subconscious minds are our "altered states," representing as they do the downward filtering of super-consciousness through the brain. Superconsciousness is our true and native state of being.

Meditation

The secret of authentic power and self-transcendence is daily, deep meditation. Meditation is the practice of communing with the depths of the intuitive within us, at the calm center of our heart. This center is the center of everything, everywhere. This is the way to attain perfect insight into people and events – into any difficulty that we face in life. This is the way of intuitive understanding.

This is also the way to cast out pain, both physical and emotional. Focus with calm feeling on your inner center, then project the center into the pain; visualize yourself at its center, and concentrate there. If you can penetrate deeply enough to its center, and send it love and light, it will cease to exist. You will find an ability to cope with any trauma. When you can understand and operate everything from your center, you will find that you can turn even major set backs in your life to good advantage.

The secret of mediation lies not in affirming states that are foreign to us, but in reclaiming what we are. Meditation is returning to our center within. It may be termed a process of upward relaxation into super-consciousness. The only "effort" required is to resist the tendency, born of habit, toward tension and restlessness. What we must do, is simply increase our receptivity – mentally and emotionally first, and then intuitively.

Meditation is not a matter of waiting passively for something to happen. We must participate in it fully for us to receive higher awareness, inspiration and guidance because we can only attain super-consciously inspired experiences on their own level of intense consciousness.

METHOD OF MEDITATION

There are many methods of meditation. For this purpose I will use a very simple method of meditation as a process of relaxing the body, quieting the mind. Messages can be projected clearly and directly into the subconscious when the conscious mind's constant barrage of multi- faceted material is stopped. When the distractions are eliminated, the different areas of the mind can be harmonized and fully focused in one direction.

Meditation is conducive to receiving knowledge and impulses from both the subconscious and the super-conscious minds. By quieting the lower minds, the way is open for the superconscious mind to reveal itself.

To meditate properly, one should find a quiet place, where one will not be disturbed for the duration of the meditation. Sit with your spine straight to stimulate energy flow. Do not cross the hands, arms, legs or feet, as this will block the circulation. Close your eye for easy concentration.

Begin to breathe deeply and rhythmically. Deep breathing establishes harmony in the mind and body. Concentrate strictly on the steady ingoing and outgoing movement of breath until you establish an even and conformable rhythm.

Next, focus your attention on each part of your body and command it to relax – starting from the top of your head to the sole of your feet. Next, command your emotions to relax by releasing all negative emotions from your emotional body. Next, command your conscious mind to relax by releasing all thought.

When the physical and emotional bodies are calm and relaxed, and the conscious mind is still and quiet, you are in a meditative state. It is then possible to communicate with both the subconscious and superconscious minds. At this stage we can also contact our higher selves, our souls and other souls in the soul plane. We will learn more about this in Chapter 18.

While in meditation we can objectively study the subconscious. We will be able to trace the cause and origin of our stumbling blocks. We can objectively observe the thoughts and memories that surface. We will be able to discover the negative images and perceptions that our problems and behavioral disorders are built upon. We can also begin to reprogram the subconscious mind with the input of new, positive information.

We can build a new and exciting future with the thoughts and images we focus on during meditation. Visualization and affirmations also work powerfully during mediation to reprogram the subconscious mind.

When we go deeper into meditation and quiet both the conscious and subconscious minds, superconscious energy will flow purely without interference. This is a process of silent listening and requires the suspension of all thoughts and emotions. The superconscious is always ready to reveal itself and will do so through impulses, ideas, insights and intuition, but the lower minds must be still and receptive. Focusing your attention on one word, or sound, or following the inflow and outflow of the breath helps clear and silence the lower minds.

Meditation is a tool through which we can realize our true nature and integrate the different states of mind. It increases one's self-awareness and capacities. In understanding and using the full power and potential of the mind, we possess the tools for controlling our own life and making the best of it.

We can also use meditation to bring cosmic energy into our lives – by imaging a beautiful white light from above flowing down through our crown chakra and filling our lives with its beautiful radiant light. Once we are filled with this infinite supply of energy we can use it to heal ourselves or send it to whomever or wherever we wish.

CHAPTER 12

THE LAW OF THINKING

"As a man thinketh in his heart so is he."
Prov. 23.7.

To most people life is an enigma, a deep mystery, a complex and incomprehensible problem, which at times appears to be hundreds of problems — but really there is only one problem: the lost child does not know the way home. Life is very simple if one only holds the key. We must recognize that mystery and apparent complexity are only other names for ignorance. All things are mysteries when they are not understood. But once we come to a full understanding of life, it no longer appears mysterious.

Prevailing Mental State of Mind

Humans are progressive beings. We are creatures of constant growth. Before us lie an unlimited ocean of possibilities to be navigated and conquered by development of our inherent powers. The human mind is the ruling factor or governing power in the entire life of man. The progress of an individual is largely determined by his/her ruling mental state. This ruling mental state regulates the actions and directions of all one's forces, faculties and powers. The sum total of our prevailing mental state will inevitably determine many of our particular experiences and our personal fate. Therefore, we have to give conscious attention at all times to our predominant mental state.

The prevailing state of mind is made up of various mental attitudes which the individual adopts towards things, events, and life in general. If we adopt an attitude which is broad in mind, optimistic in tone and true to life, our prevailing mental state will correspond and exhibit a highly constructive and progressive tendency.

The conscious mind controls all the forces of our personality in one way or another; it is also largely responsible for our daily physical and mental states. Hence it is obvious that the prevailing mental state of an individual will determine the direction in which one's powers are to proceed.

If our prevailing mental state is aspiring, harmonious, and positive, all our forces will be directed into constructive channels. However, if our prevailing mental state of mind is discordant and negative, then almost all our forces will be misdirected. Of all the factors that regulate the life and experience of human beings, none exercises a greater influence than our prevailing state of mind.

Our mental attitudes are the results of ideas which have their origin in our point of view and our beliefs. By seeking a true and natural point of view we can secure the best and most superior point of view, which will determine our prevailing state of mind.

We Do Not See With Our Eyes

There is a lot of truth to the statement "believing is seeing". As human beings we are prone to believe more than we can see. Still there are some people who will only accept the evidence of the senses, but we shall come to realize more and more that it is what we believe that determines what we shall see. Then we will realize that many of our defeats and failures are due to our mental blindness, not to our moral deviations.

If we should live only by our physical sight, our world would be very small. In fact our world would consist of only what we can see or have seen. Also if we were to believe in the testimony of our eyes we would accept many conditions that are not true. For example, if you stand on a beach and watch a ship sail away, it will come to a point where it appears to have sunk under the water. This is not true. The ship was not sinking even though our physical senses tell us differently. Therefore when you are worried over some obstacle or problem, you must remind yourself that it may be purely an illusion of the senses, that it may not be true at all according to the laws of nature.

Our eyes are like a pair of windows; at the back of the window there is a reflector and this reflector forms an image of what we see and sets up a wave current. This wave current follows along thin wires called nerves which relay the image to the brain, which is referred to as the memory center. If the picture is a common one our memory accepts it readily, but if we are looking upon some new scene, our memory does not recognize it, and then we must repeat the picture over and over many times until it makes a lasting impression. Hence we do not see with our eyes; rather we see with our minds.

What is Thought

Thought is a subtle element, an actual force or substance; it is a thing as real as electricity, light, heat, water or even stone; although it is invisible to the physical sight. We are surrounded by a vast ocean of thought substance through which our thoughts pass like currents of electricity, or tiny streaks of light or musical waves. We can flash our thought completely around the world many times in less than a single second.

Scientifically, thought travels at a faster rate of speed than light, which travels at the speed of 186,000 miles per second or 930,000 times faster than the sound of our voices. It is a proven scientific fact that the mind is a battery of forces, the greatest of any known element.

Thought is an unlimited force. Our power to think is inexhaustible, yet very few of us are fully aware of the possibilities of our thought power. We are mere infants when it comes to handling thought power. As we grow in the understanding and in the right use of thoughts, we will learn to banish our ills, to establish good in every form we may desire. It is our power to think that determines our state of living.

As we think, we generate a power far and near, which sets up a radiation and vibration which becomes individual as we determine it. Our thoughts affect our welfare and affect what we think of. The kind of thoughts we think, attract the same kind of conditions. For example, if we take the thought of success and keep it in mind, the thought elements will attract success to us, for in the spiritual world like attracts like.

If we think success we will be mentally drawn to the universal thought currents of success as these thought currents of success are in existence all around us. We will psychically contact minds who think along the same lines and later those minds will be brought into our lives. Success minded people help success to come to them. This is how successful living is found.

The law of mind is in perpetual operation, and it works both ways. People who dwell on thoughts of failure or poverty will gravitate towards like conditions. They will draw to them people who accept failure and poverty. Alternatively, we can think on positive conditions, on success and plenty, and in the same manner enjoy full and plenty. Whatever the mind holds within takes form in the outer world.

ONE FORCE

Many people think that there are two forces and that we must deal with them separately. That is, to attract the good we must do away with the bad. This is not true. For example, if we are cold, we do not work with cold and heat alike in order to get warm. Instead, we build a fire, and we gather around that fire, we enjoy the heat that is emanated from it and become warm. As we build up warmth the cold disappears for cold is the absence of heat. To be warm we give our whole thought to those things which tend to create warmth. We ignore the cold in thinking of heat and bring forth heat.

We must understand that prosperity and poverty are not two things; they are merely two sides of the same thing. They are but one power rightly or wrongly used. We cannot think of plenty and then worry about the unfavourable conditions that may seem imminent. When we think of plenty, lack, its opposite, will disappear. All our thoughts must be directed to that one thing which we desire in order that our desire may be fulfilled.

The process is not manipulating two powers, not dealing with good and evil, right and wrong, prosperity and poverty, but by following the law of good and dwelling upon that which is good, we shall bring to pass all good things.

The mind force is creating continually. Like fertile soil nature does not differentiate between the seed of weed and that of flower. Nature produces and causes both seeds to grow. The same energy is used for both and so is the mind. The mind creates either good or bad, our ideas determine which is to be nurtured and grow.

Fear

Whatever we fear will come upon us. Our thoughts will surely bring into our reality the fears that we subconsciously entertained and accepted. Our fears can do so much to us that we should be very careful what we fear and worry about. Fear is the greatest enemy of mankind. Fear has a tendency to break down a person's mental resistance and make him/her more susceptible to diseases.

The world is realizing more and more that we dare not entertain in our minds any fear lest it come upon us. Whatever we think in our minds must grow. If some condition handicaps us; perhaps a weed that must be plucked out, it is important to know that the condition is the effect that we see; it is not the cause that we see. We have to weed out all the bad thoughts and replace them with good thoughts.

> If it is fear replace it with courage
> If it is disease replace it with health
> If it is lack replace it with plenty.

We can do this by being disciplined, and alter or change the trend of our thoughts. As we change our thoughts to the good and positive the negative thoughts will disappear on their own.

As long as we allow something to seem real to us, we are putting our energy into it. We are nurturing it; we are feeding it; we are keeping it alive; we are putting our faith into that thing. Whether we like it or not, it must naturally grow, for the law of growth is ever working to produce whatever seed we plant. Man can impress his thought on formless substance and cause the thing he thinks about to be created.

Cause and Effect

We are constantly thinking: we can change our thoughts, but we cannot stop thinking. The thinking power flows in and through us like the very air we breathe. Our challenge therefore, is to direct our power of thinking into constructive channels of expression. It is a scientific fact that no power can act without producing some type of effect, and by merely thinking we are continually producing effects. These effects register and record in our daily lives. When our thoughts are aimless and imperfect, we create for ourselves pain and confusion. This is misdirected energy.

The first question in our self development is: are we controlled by our thoughts? Or are we controlling our thoughts?

Are we using our thoughts for gain? Or are our thoughts using us for continued loss?

Disciplined State of Mind

"Seek ye first the kingdom of heaven and all things shall be added unto you". What is heaven? Heaven is a state of mind; it is an orderly, disciplined, constructive state of thinking. Therefore to gain all things, we must gain a disciplined, orderly, constructive state of mind.

Have you a disciplined mind? Have you any dominating appetite? Are you emotional? Do you vent your feelings through impatience, temper, malice, hate, pride, envy, conceit, lies, dishonesty and the like?

We must realize that if any of these negations are controlling our lives it will prevent or delay good from coming to us. Anything in life that controls us, makes us a servant to its dictate and blocks expression of our authentic power. All our weakness and our lacks are due to some compelling influence that blinds us and keeps from us what we naturally would receive, if we were free in mind to receive them.

Power of the Human Being

We are endowed with the power to overcome all mistakes and evil forces. This power is unfailing in its operation. When used properly, we can master any trial. Nature has no problems it cannot solve; it has no troubles it cannot remove; all its movements are governed by the law of order and discipline. We can say and do the same if we will pattern ourselves after nature.

Thought in our mind is governed by the same exactness as nature. The law of thought is as simple as the law of gravity. That is, if a stone is thrown in the air it will fall to the ground. Mind is the source and the cause of conditions, situations and circumstances in our lives; therefore, we must start to adjust and discipline our thoughts in order to stabilize our affairs.

The fact that every problem is mental is another reason why we must learn to control our thoughts in order to determine our lives. We must recognize that our problems are mental. For example, if we desire to get rich, we find that wealth is not a place or an environment, for people in the same environment are both rich and poor. Neither are riches due to any particular business, for people in the same business are poor and rich alike. Rather riches are due to something in the minds of the people that make the wealth, and that something in the mind, is the quality and type of thoughts their minds entertain.

Organized Discernment

Nature has every movement well organized. A cut plant soon wilts and dies because it has been taken away from the source of its life. Also a hungry lion in the jungle does not roar and lash out in order to find his prey. Instead, instinct warns the lion to be quiet, to steal carefully upon his prey, to stalk his meal. It is the same instinct which allows a cat to wait patiently for hours to catch a mouse.

These are examples of organized action that are instinctive in animals. We must adhere to this instinct. This is the organized method, the constructive method. A disorganized method will be destructive and negative. We must stalk our success or any other worthwhile enterprise in the same way as the lion who stalks his meal. We must work ourselves up to gain success; it does not just fall into our lap.

To just roar or to shout our statement is not enough. Birds of dollars will not fall out of the tree by our disorganized noise — through fright, they will more likely fly away. When our ideas are organized they are under our control. We have to arrange our thoughts in such a way that they work together as a single unit. Our mind must be controlled in its expression so that every process of thought will be in an orderly fashion.

All our action is the result of thought and will. It determines our conditions in life, and to have better conditions in life we must first make efforts to organize our thoughts.

Most people wish to gain the best in life but they do not know how to think correctly. The average person thinks randomly, with no clear design in the mind to frame the thoughts. Thus the average person's thinking is beyond control, chaotic, and unorganized. This is why disappointment and failures are always near, for they flounder in indecision.

We attract into our lives only what we think or create; this is the law of thinking. To achieve success we must first think it, we must work it, we must become it. To advance we must think it and make some effort to rise. To obtain happiness we must train our mind to adapt our thoughts and lives to the law of harmony, order and peace. To rise above any limitation we must organize our thinking along constructive lines.

The law of thinking is simple and practical. For example, if you want to climb a mountain, you don't sit at the bottom wishing, hoping and waiting for some force to come and carry you to the mountain top. Instead you organize your thoughts and decide that you are going to climb the mountain, you gather the tools and ingredients that you are going to need and you start climbing. You would climb steadily, keeping your eyes on the target: the mountain top. You may wind around; you may slip back a step or two; you may even fall; maybe even stop and rest for a while; but you keep your thoughts collected and your desired intent upon reaching the mountain top and you will eventually get there. There is no other way.

All our problems are due to the fact that we are not controlling our ideas and the way we think. Nature has no problem because she it? is orderly and disciplined. Self control consists of an organized thought direction; that is, we start out with a well defined aim or objective, think about it continuously, not just for thirty minutes, plan our time and work so that we are working steadily towards our goal.

We must fill our day with constructive duties so that there will be no room for idle chatter or waste of any kind to enter. This development will enable us to move steadily upward toward success. When our thoughts are in order, problems will cease to be perplexing and mysterious. We must allow knowledge and understanding to supplant fear and ignorance, and that which was invisible will become visible, that which was unknown will become known. Then life with its circumstances is no longer an enigma, but a clear interpretation of the law of thinking. We are what we are because of our state of thinking. We attract only what we think and create.

PART IV

THE EMOTIONAL

The Nature of Emotions
The Inner Child
Overcoming Our Fears
Interdependence

CHAPTER 13

THE NATURE OF OUR EMOTIONS

*The essence of our being is love. Only
love exists — everything else is an illusion.*

Many of us have chosen to repress and cripple the growth of our emotional nature. This neglect is universal; many of us look mainly after our physical selves. We do more or less what is necessary to make it grow and remain healthy. Some choose to cultivate the mental side as well. In order to do so we learn to use our brain, our thinking capacity; we absorb, we train our memory and our logical reasoning capability. All this aids mental growth.

Why is the emotional nature generally neglected? There are good reasons for this; to gain more clarity let us first understand the function of the emotional nature in human beings. It includes the capacity to feel. We avoid or ignore our emotions because we fear being vulnerable. The capacity to experience feelings is synonymous with the capacity to give and receive love and happiness. To the degree we shy away from any kind of emotional experience, to that extent we also close the door to the experience of love and happiness.

Our emotions represent one of the most powerful doors to our soul. There is an incredible wealth and richness in the gift of our emotions, which we are yet to acknowledge, understand and use appropriately. While our intellect is closely linked to our outer life, our emotions are closely linked to our inner life. Importantly, our emotions have the ability to move through and experience many different states of awareness. Emotion is the key to our human growth, development and evolution; it is through our emotions what we connect to our higher selves and spiritual selves.

Emotion is essential to understanding spirituality because emotions generate feelings. The mental aspect is linked to our physical body, while our emotional aspect is linked to our spiritual aspect. The spiritual body is of course the body that exists beyond physical limitations; our emotions are our tools to comprehend the non-physical reality. Many of us don't want to go beyond our emotions or personal boundaries because it might be painful.

Most of us would like to be free from feelings and pain. We are afraid of our emotional or feeling center. We are afraid to feel. We must learn to trust our feelings no matter what they are. Trust that they lead to something and that the way we feel is necessary for our present level of growth. Most of us want to be in life and then be removed from it at the same time. We say, "let me just be here and be a powerful person but I don't want to feel or participate because it hurts too much."

When we are no longer afraid of our feelings, we will move past judgment and allow ourselves to feel. We will experience a tremendous breakthrough, because we will be able to ride feelings into other realities. Some of us are afraid to feel and to participate in this reality, let alone other realities because we do not trust our feelings. If we wish to have accelerated drive along the pathway into authentic power then we must stop skirting the issue of feeling and face our feelings, no matter what they are.

It is not that we don't know how to feel, it's more that we are afraid of our feelings. We don't know what to do with them when we have them; they bring up a sense of powerlessness within us, so that we associate negative feeling with a sense of "Oh no I blew it". We have a boundary in our belief system that states that when something comes up that is emotional and brings pain or anger — then it is not good, it is time to stop, to turn around, avoid, deny and judge our emotions. There is a purpose to these moments, because they carry important messages to help us grow to the next step in our evolution.

Purpose of Emotions

We must learn to face our negative emotions directly, to walk through them and deal with them head on. We must find out why an emotion is in our life and to actually recognise that this emotion is there to teach us something. Your emotional body can be compared to your physical body. For example, if you have a physical pain such as a toothache, and you ignore it, over time it will only get worse, because it is there to alert you that something is wrong with your tooth and that it needs your attention. Likewise, if you ignore your emotional pain it will also get worse because it is there to alert you to something that is wrong with your emotional body or your life.

Even anger serves a purpose. If you feel angry – don't try to deny it, instead acknowledge it. Say, "Hey, I am feeling angry". Feel the anger and be with the anger, and work through the anger. Ask yourself, "why does this person or this circumstance make me angry?" "What lesson is here for me to learn from feeling anger in this particular situation?" "What growth opportunity is here for me?" "What does this person or circumstance remind me of that I have not yet healed in my life?" Once we approach our anger with this type of consciousness we will find that we will learn the lesson very quickly and the fear and anger will dissipate.

Most of us want to be finished with our emotion, to sweep it under the rug and act as if it is no good. We act like it is a rotten vegetable, as if there is no purpose to it — throw it out and bury it in the back yard. There is a purpose to fear and there is a purpose to anger. For example, fear and anger can bring our consciousness to stimulus that triggers that kind of emotional response or reaction. If we would allow ourselves to express and experience our fears, which might lead to the expression of our anger, we would learn something crucial to our growth. Those of us who want desperately to avoid fear and anger and who are really afraid of these feelings, have something great to learn through these negative emotions. They are techniques that move us beyond our personal boundaries of identity and self-image and allow us to work through our emotional triggers.

We are simply afraid to experience our emotions most of the time — all of us want to be accepted. We feel that no one will like us if we do certain things or feel certain ways, so we don't give ourselves permission to have those feelings. That is where our anger comes from. We have anger because we make judgments about what we can and cannot do. If we do not give ourselves permission to feel we cannot learn. Feelings connect us with life and other dimensions.

Feelings serve a variety of purposes in our lives. Therefore, we must trust, cultivate and rely on our feelings. We must understand that our feelings are our ticket to ride into the spiritual, multidimensional and multi-sensory reality. In multi-sensory and multidimensional realities we learn to hold and focus many different versions of ourselves. Only feelings can take us to these places, particularly feelings that we trust. Many of us are very suspicious about our feelings. We will not allow certain feelings to come forward or we judge them when they come up instead of observing where they will take us or what they do for us.

Because we fear something we keep ourselves from experiencing it. We put up a wall that says, "if I go there it is bad". We put the brakes on. Our fear will eventually energize the experience into our realm of development because all thought is drawn into form based on the emotional experience behind it. When we feel fear or anger the best thing to do is to simply say; "what the heck, I will go there, I will surrender," then deal with being there and don't worry about not being centered while we are experiencing the feeling. If we intend on always being in control while we are in our feelings we will not give ourselves the range of movement that is needed to ride the emotion that knocks down boundaries and belief systems.

Anger is not purposeless and pain is not purposeless. They both lead into something. You can make an intention to go into your feeling center and learn how to be centered there while you explore the opportunities there. Going into your emotional body and intending to have centeredness does not mean that things won't fluctuate. It means that you allow things to fluctuate; you ride it, then you get out of it. You will either experience a calm ride or a rough ride. But the ride is necessary for you to learn what you need to learn. If you avoid or ignore the emotional ride, the opportunity will keep coming back to teach you what you need to learn. There is no way to ignore or avoid life.

Our emotions are connected with our spiritual body. We may want to bypass something that is difficult, yet we have to feel our way through it. We have to go through our emotional body to reach our spiritual body. There is no way to bypass our emotional body; therefore we must learn to deal with feelings and emotions appropriately. We want to sweep the difficult things under the carpet and say, "I don't want to deal with these things", not realizing that these difficult things are our gemstones.

Even if you discover that you have a hundred thousand boundaries, do not feel frustrated, simply say, "this is interesting". Look at the boundaries you have set up and instead of swearing at them, simply observe them and see if you can discover how they came about. See what purpose they serve. As soon as we acknowledge, recognize and are willing to deal with our emotions, they move; when we cling to or have fear of any emotion or say; "I like that boundary, it serves me well," then we limit ourselves.

Our emotions are not just food for others, they are food for ourselves as well. When we trust others we are feeding and trusting ourselves. When we forgive others we are feeding and forgiving ourselves. When we love others we are feeding and loving ourselves. This is how we nourish ourselves and create a positive identity. Emotions feed us and feed our identity into existence through our emotional body.

Feelings and Control

Most of us want to control our feelings at all cost. We try to manipulate life in such a way that will create or recreate feelings that we experienced sometime in the past. We spend our lives trying to get back lost love relationships, trying to recreate past happiness or trying to relive old pleasures. This is our attempt at trying to control life. We try to do this because we are fearful of our feelings.

We must learn to trust our emotions. As long as we describe something as difficult we are making it difficult. We insist on resisting and judging the changes that our higher selves bring in our lives to facilitate our growth and transformation. One's ego feels that it doesn't know what is going on and it wishes to be in control. Control can be something very convenient and very handy, but it must be applied at the right place and at the right time. It's kind of like super glue. Glue in a wrong place doesn't do any good. For example, you can glue your hands or your lips together, which would be no good. We must learn to exercise control in the way we use glue. If we screw up with glue we get stuck and we can't do anything. Control is the same way. We get stuck with it and it sticks. We can get stuck to something we don't want to be stuck to. We must be very selective about what we decide to control or not control. The old paradigm is that we must be in control of everything. This is wrong; we must be selective in control.

We should not resist and feel out of control because we don't know what is coming and it appears that our emotions are getting in our way. Our emotions just simply want to show us something. Our emotional center operates just like the oil lamp in our car; when we are experiencing positive emotions all is well with us, and when we are experiencing negative emotions, we need to stop and take a reality check. We don't like it because we think our emotions are interfering, getting in our way or will allow us to embarrass ourselves. Get clever next time you come into one of these emotional situations. Say to yourself, "I know what is going on. I am not getting caught in this one. I know there is something there for me to learn and something there for me to change. I believe that I am guided and that I am following a blueprint; so I will check out what is in this for me by not judging it and by going with the flow."

Consciousness and Emotion

We can become conscious and aware of how we respond and react emotionally to stimuli in our environment. When we experience an emotional trigger, instead of reacting from our habitual emotional reactions, we can stop and create a gap between the stimulus and the reaction and consciously allow a responsible emotional response to materialize. If someone insults you, instead of feeling sad and disturbed, you can choose to create a gap between the insult and your emotional response. In that gap you can use your consciousness to allow additional and different emotional responses to come forth. In the gap you may choose to express love and compassion for the other person and yourself.

We can also choose to examine the origin of our habitual

emotional responses and empower ourselves by allowing additional or different emotional responses. We all have set emotions for particular situations and circumstances, which have been instilled in us from our culture and experiences. For example, if someone insults you, you may feel sad or disturbed. While if someone compliments you, you may feel happy and accepted. When we become balanced and centered, the comments, behavior or actions of others will not affect our emotional state.

We can also consciously intend that all our growth and changes come in joy, peace and harmony. But for that to happen we must learn to trust our emotions. We will have to go with the energy and see what is changing for us and what we need to give up. If we have not cultivated trust inside ourselves, we will shut down because we don't understand what is happening. When we are ready for change it is imperative that we trust our feeling center, for feeling is what will lead us in the right direction.

We must become friendly with our emotions because it is through our feelings that we can climb the ladder into multisensory and multidimensional realities. Through feelings we can detect subtle frequency changes. For example, you may be in a room with three people and a fourth person walks in and all of a sudden you experience a change in the frequency in the room. Your mind will say, "oh it's nothing", but you know for sure that you felt something. Your logical mind will dis-involve itself when frequency changes take place. Feelings register frequency changes; logical mind does not.

Our feelings are our essence, our jewels, our treasure, and our gems from which we can learn about our identity. They are our springboards; we are never finished with them. We cannot shove them away and say, "I don't like them".

We also need to honor our friends as they go through their stuff. We must not get involved in their stuff. We can honor and send them positive energy, but don't help them prolong their drama. It is wise to move through stuff, not to create a 365-day soap opera. Some of us just love melodramas – everyday we are either repeating the same melodrama or creating a new one. We can tell our story once, twice or even three times at the most and be done with it. We don't need to tell everyone everything because everyone else has his or her own stuff occurring as well.

When we continually speak about ourselves, we are missing the point, because we are talking instead of being and feeling. What we are doing by talking to everyone about what is going on with us is simply wanting to get attention and we don't need to do that. Events are ongoing and we never really finish with them because they are our stuff. They stay with us until we grow past them and then new stuff comes up for us to deal with. There is no end to stuff that we have to deal with.

If something is painful for us at the time and we avoid it, it will come back later to haunt us. If, however, we go through the pain and later we encounter a similar situation we will have gained knowledge, experience and compassion that we never had before. We will see the situation from a different perspective. Suppressed emotions are the main things that block us from perceiving reality. They are the parts of our emotional body where the highway system was severed and the information could not flow. So we move into emotional pain and translate the emotional pain out into our physical body.

We will have to learn to bring emotional energy from outside the cosmo into our bodies. Infusing it with our other bodies; mental, physical, emotional and spiritual. When you allow energy to infuse your being and to come into your body the energy moves through our chakra system (energy centers) and feeds our body. When we are afraid or we shut down or when we blame someone else or when we are in denial, we get stuck. Even though energy flows, it does not fit, so we experience chaos and everyone else wants to stay away from us because we emanate chaos. Chaos is a fine place to be. There is nothing wrong with chaos as long as we don't permanently dwell there.

DENYING AND NEGLECTING OUR EMOTIONS

In my experiential training courses I often incorporate exercises that involve participants reporting on the feelings they had during the exercise. I am often struck by the resistance and denial some of the participants have in acknowledging their feelings and bringing them to a conscious level. When we deny our emotions they do not go away, they simply boil up like a volcano waiting to explode in one way or another. For example, if you are sad and angry and you deny that, you may pretend to be happy, but you will not be empowered to go to the source and heal your sadness and anger; thus you will not grow or change. And eventually it will explode and you will find yourself doing crazy and angry things and later asking yourself why.

When we deny our emotions we are asking for major blockages to take place within our physical, emotional, mental and spiritual bodies. We could experience significant malfunctioning in our physical bodies. We could experience heart and other problems in our internal organs. However, when we allow our feelings to manifest we will experience a little discomfort here and there, but usually no major volcanoes or hurricanes. We will be allowing our emotions freedom of expression and they will not run rampant over our personal environment. They simply occur and move on.

Feelings are what connect our mind and body to our spiritual body. Our emotions are our key to being alive in this reality. In this reality emotions are our greatest gifts. If we deny our emotional self then we had best realize that we have "hung it up". If you are not going to be part of your emotional self then you are never going to experience your authentic power or achieve your full human potential. You will simply be one of the masses who watch television and feel like a victim over and over again.

If you are feeling pain within your emotional body ask yourself why you believe the pain is there, what purpose the pain serves and why you are choosing to create pain through your emotions. Why is it not your choice to create joy instead? Remember it is your choice, consciously or unconsciously.

In order to know ourselves on a deep level it becomes increasingly necessary to allow all emotions to reach surface awareness so as to understand and enable them to mature. Most of us have a great resistance to letting this happen and are unaware of the obstructions we put in the way of our own growth. Hence it is necessary that we discuss the mechanism of our resistance.

Human beings who function harmoniously have developed the physical, mental, emotional and spiritual sides of their nature. These forces are supposed to function harmoniously with one another, each helping the other, rather than one faculty subduing another. If one function is underdeveloped it causes disharmony in the human structure and also cripples the entire personality.

Moreover, the emotional side of our nature, when functioning, possesses creative ability. To the degree we close ourselves off from emotional experience our full potential and our creative ability is hindered. The unfolding of creative ability is not a mere mental process; in fact, the intellect has much less to do with it than may appear at first glance. In spite of the fact that technical skills require the mental process, our creativity is an intuitive process. Our intuition can function only to the degree that our emotional life is strong, healthy and mature. Our intuitive powers will be hindered if we have neglected emotional growth and discouraged ourselves from experiencing the world of feeling.

Emotions and Happiness

In the world of feeling we experience the good and the bad, the happy and the unhappy, pleasure and pain. Rather than just registering such impressions mentally, emotional experiences really touch us. Since our struggle is primarily for happiness and since immature emotions lead to unhappiness, our secondary aim comes with the avoidance of unhappiness. Unhappy circumstances exist. In every child's life pain and disappointments are common. This creates the early most unconscious conclusion "If I do not feel then I will not be unhappy."

Instead of taking courageous and appropriate steps — of living through negative, immature emotions in order to afford them the opportunity to grow and thus become mature and constructive — the childish emotions are suppressed. They are put out of awareness and buried so that they remain inadequate and destructive even though we may be unaware of the existence. Although it is true that we can shut down our capacity for emotional experience and therefore not feel immediate pain, it is also true that we simultaneously dull our capacity for happiness and pleasure.

While avoiding the dreaded unhappiness may seem attractive in the short run, in the long run the unhappiness we seek to avoid will come to us in a different and much more painful but indirect way. The bitter hurt of isolation, of loneliness, of the feeling of having passed through life without experiencing its heights and depths, without developing ourselves to the most and best we can be, is the result of such a wrong choice. Using such evasive tactics we do not experience life at its fullest.

By attempting to withdraw from pain, we withdraw from happiness, and most of all from the experience of life. We withdraw from living, loving and experiencing, from everything that makes life rich and rewarding. The result is that our intuitive powers are dulled, together with our creative faculties; we only function at a fraction of our human potential.

The damage we have inflicted upon ourselves with the pseudo-solution, and continue inflicting upon ourselves as long as we adhere to it, is one that eludes our comprehension. Somewhere deep inside we hope and believe that it is possible to love and to be loved while we dull our world of feeling into a state of numbness and thereby prohibit ourselves from truly loving. We will not experience authentic love, power, belonging or communication if we neither feel nor express the occasional glimpses of feelings that we strive for.

Since we protect ourselves in this foolish manner, we isolate ourselves, which means exposing ourselves much more to that which we are trying to avoid. Hence we miss out doubly. We cannot avoid that which we fear, and in the long run we also miss out on all we could have if we had not run away from living. For living and feeling are one and the same.

The love and fulfillment we must increasingly crave and don't get, makes us blame others, circumstances and events instead of seeing how we are responsible for our own unhappiness. We resist such insight because we sense that the moment we see it fully, we will have to change and we can no longer cling to the comfortable but unrealizable hope that we can have what we want without meeting the necessary conditions to get it. If you want happiness you must be willing to give it. How can you give it, if you are unwilling and unable to feel as much as you are capable of feeling? Realize that it is you who causes the state of your fulfillment and it is you who can still change it.

MATURE VS. IMMATURE EMOTIONS

Emotional expression can be mature and constructive or immature and destructive. As a child you possess an immature body and mind and therefore quite naturally an immature emotional structure. Most of us gave our body and mind a chance to grow out of immaturity and to reach a certain physical and mental maturity. We allow our body to grow; we allow our mind to grow, however we stop our emotional self from growing and functioning, because we are afraid of our emotions. We not only hinder experiences as a result of this reasoning, but we also hinder all the transitory functioning that alone can lead to constructive mature emotions.

Since this is more or less the case with every one of us, the growth period of experiencing and maturing emotionally has to happen now in our adulthood. There is much less resistance in human nature to the necessary growing pains of the physical and mental sides of the personality than to the growth of the emotional nature. Hardly anyone recognizes that emotional growing pains are necessary too and that they are constructive and beneficial. Without consciously thinking about it in these terms we believe that the emotional growth process should come about without growing pains. Most of the time we completely ignore that this area exists at all, let alone that it needs growth and development. Neither do we know how much growth is to be accomplished.

If we understand this, our resistance will finally give way and we will no longer object with going through a period of growth. Now we must allow our immature feelings to surface in this growing period. Immature emotions have to express themselves. Not only are they allowed expressions for the purpose of understanding their significance but also the opportunity for us to learn important lessons. We will finally reach a point when we no longer need such immature emotions.

When we were hurt as a child our reactions were anger, resentment and pain, sometimes to a very strong degree. If we prevent ourselves now from consciously experiencing these emotions we will not get rid of them. We will not enable healthy mature emotions to follow in their place but we will simply repress existing immature feelings. We will bury them and try deceiving ourselves that we do not feel what we actually feel. Since we dull our capacity we become unaware of what exists underneath. We superimpose feelings that we think we ought to have but that we do not really and truly have.

The act of being aware of our immature emotional feelings must be distinguished from giving vent or action to them. I am not saying that you should go out and act out your emotional feelings. I am simply saying that we should be aware of them because if we are not aware of them it does not mean that they are not there. They are still there, it's just that we are denying them and we are covering them and then they can be even more destructive to our spiritual and emotional growth. In that sense when we become aware of them, we can talk about them and deal with them in an appropriate setting that will clear them out of the way and create an opportunity for us to replace them with mature emotional feelings.

As we take a few steps in the direction of becoming aware of what we feel and express in an indirect way without finding excuses, we will gain understanding about ourselves such as we have never had before. We will not only come to understand what brings on many unwelcome results but how we have the power to change them. Understanding the interaction between others and ourselves will show us how our subconscious mind distorts facts and affects others in the opposite way to that which we originally intended. This will give us an inner understanding about the process and importance of communication especially on an emotional level.

This is the only way that emotions can mature, by going through the period that was missed in childhood and adolescence. The emotions will finally mature and we will no longer need to fear the inner power that we believe we cannot control, by merely putting them out of our awareness. We will be able to trust them and be guided by them for that is the final aim of the mature and well functioning person.

When healthy emotions make our intuition reliable there will be mutual harmony between the mental and emotional faculties. One will not contradict the other. As long as we cannot rely on our intuitive process we will be insecure and lacking in self-confidence. We try to make up for this by relying on others or on false religion; this makes us weak and helpless. But if we have mature and strong emotions we will trust ourselves and find a security we never dreamt possible.

We all want to grow spiritually. However, many of us want to accomplish spiritual growth without accomplishing emotional growth. This is completely impossible. We will have to make up our minds whether we really want emotional growth or we still want to cling to the childish hope that spiritual growth is possible while we neglect the world of feeling and allow it to lie dormant without giving it the opportunity to grow.

LOVE AND EMOTION

Love is the first and the greatest power. In the final analysis it is the only power. How can we love if we do not let ourselves feel? How can we love and at the same time remain detached emotionally? That means remaining personally uninvolved, not risking pain, disappointment, or personal involvement. Can we love in such a comfortable way, numbing our faculty of feelings? How can we truly experience love? Is love an intellectual process? Is love a lukewarm matter of law, words, regulations and rules we talk about or is love a feeling that comes from deep within our soul? Love is warmth of flowing impact that cannot leave us indifferent and untouched.

Love is foremost a feeling and only after the feeling is fully experienced and expressed will wisdom and perhaps even intellectual insight as a by-product result from it. How can we hope to gain spirituality – and spirituality and love are one — by neglecting our emotional process? Think about this and begin to see how we all sit back hoping for a comfortable spirituality that leaves out our personal involvement in the world of feelings. After we feel this clearly we will comprehend how preposterous this attitude is.

Our conscious and unconscious rationalization is still denying the awareness and expressions of our emotions, even though they are at the moment still destructive. Any spiritual development is a farce if we deny this part of our being. If we do not have the courage to allow the negative in us to reach our surface awareness how can healthy, strong emotions fill our being? If we cannot deal with the negative awareness, the very same negative awareness will stand in the way of the positive.

When we first start to explore all our feelings and do what is so necessary we will first experience a host of negative feelings. After these are dealt with and properly understood, mature, constructive feelings will evolve. We will feel warmth, compassion and good involvement such as we never felt possible. We will no longer feel ourselves isolated from each other. We will begin to relate to others in truth and in reality, not in falsehood, deception or self-deception. When this happens a new security and respect for ourselves will become part of us. We will begin to trust and love ourselves, thus enabling ourselves to trust and love others.

CHAPTER 14

THE INNER CHILD

*We all have an inner child – if we are not
aware of it and control it, it will control
our lives.*

Every single human being in this world still harbors an attitude of fear and weakness within themselves. This corner of our personality usually induces strong hurt, guilt or shame. It is kept secret, often even from the awareness of our conscious mind. We invent many different devices in order to hide this weakness and dependency that make us feel utterly helpless, unable to assert ourselves and even unable to protect our truth, honor and integrity. This area of our personality will constantly compel us to sell out and betray our authentic power, in order to ward off disapproval, censure and rejection. We don't even realize that the need to be accepted by others is sometimes less shameful than the means to which our ego resorts to placate and appease others.

Nothing robs our authentic power and gives us inner pain and shame as this inner, fearful, weak spot that makes us feel impotent and compelled to sell out. This area of our personality has remained an immature inner child. This inner child does not yet know that the whole of the personality has grown up and is indeed no longer helpless and dependent. Infants and young children truly are helpless and dependent on their parent. But in the childish corner of our being, we either do not know or do not want to know that this is no longer true.

The young child is dependent on parents for all the basics of life, such as shelter, food, protection and for the necessary supply of love and pleasure. A human being cannot live without love and pleasure. To deny this truth is one of the most harmful errors. Body, soul, mind and spirit wither without love and pleasure. As adults we are able to find through our own effort and resources our own shelter, food, affection and safety, so we are also able to do the same with love and pleasure. In all of these areas we must have contact, cooperation and communication with others in varying degrees to be successful. We cannot provide ourselves with any of these necessities without interaction with other people. The mature adult interaction is however, entirely different from the passive, weak, dependent interaction of the small child.

The mature adult person uses his or her own best endowments, such as intellect, intuition, talent, observation and flexibility to get along with others in giving and receiving. Our adult sense of fairness makes us sufficiently pliable to give in, while our healthy sense of self makes us sufficiently assertive not to be stepped on and to be abused. The often-fine balance in these forces of communication can not be taught — it can only come through personal growth and development.

Infants and young children are incapable of achieving this balance. Children must have their parents' permission to establish and utilize the source of all pleasure deep within themselves. Through the parents' guidance and permission the child will develop the strength and security to make meaningful contact with others. When we need another person's permission to experience pleasure, we are still in the position of a child or infant.

When part of our development is arrested, we wait for another person, a parent substitute, to make it possible for us to draw on the deep source of our own rich feelings. We know of and yearn for these pleasurable feelings, but this part of us does not know that we are no longer a child, dependent on others for being allowed to activate and express them.

To deny the intense pleasure of being, the pleasure of feeling the energy flow of our body, soul, and spirit, is to deny life. When a child suffers such denial, his or her psyche seems to be in a shock from the repeated absence of pleasure and therefore the repeated presence of unfulfilled yearning. The shock prevents growth in this one area, so that the whole personality grows lopsidedly. Our adult conscious mind ignores the fact that a crying, demanding, and helpless child still exists within us. We do not know that we are free to move towards pleasure, towards our own fulfillment, towards the realization of our own power to obtain whatever we want and need. This is one of the most fundamental splits in human personality.

This is our human tragedy, for we just moved into a vicious cycle. Whenever a misconception is accepted as truth, immediately a vicious cycle comes into being, paralyzing the pleasure forces, which is a good part of the energy available to us. Our life thus becomes dull and lusterless.

The Vicious Cycle

When we do not know that everything in the universe already exists and that we can manifest everything we need in our own lives, we feel dependent on an outside force or authority for all we want and need. This distortion of the facts causes us to wait for this fulfillment from the wrong source. Such waiting keeps our needs perpetually unfulfilled. The more unfulfilled it is the more urgent the need becomes. The more urgent the need, the greater the dependency, and the more frantic we attempt to please the other who is supposed to fill our needs. We then become demanding and desperate. The more we try, the less we fill our needs, precisely because our attempts are misdirected and unrealistic.

Consciously we know none of this; we do not know what

force drives us or even what direction we are driven. We become desperate, because, in our urgency to have the need fulfilled we betray our truth, integrity, purpose, destiny and ourselves. Our frustrated striving and our self-betrayal create a vicious cycle, which in turn creates a forcing-current.

This forcing-current may manifest in very subtle ways and may not be overt or conscious at all, but emotions are all cramped up with it. Any forcing-current is bound to make others resist and shrink back, even if what they are forced to do is for their own benefit and delight. Thus the vicious cycle continues. The continued frustration, which we believe to be caused by the other person's refusal to co-operate and to give us what we want, brings into our lives rage, fury, even vindictiveness and varying degrees of cruel impulses. This, in turn, weakens the personality even more as guilt comes up. We conclude that these destructive feelings must be hidden so as not to antagonize this other person whom we perceive as the source of our pleasure.

The net of entanglement becomes tighter and tighter; the individual is completely caught in the trap of misconceptions, distortions and illusions with all the destructive emotions that follow suit. We find ourselves in the preposterous position of craving the love and acceptance of a person whom we hate and at the same time resenting them for having left us unfulfilled for so long. This one-sided insistence on being loved by a person we deeply resent and wish to punish increases the guilt. For the ever wakeful presence of our real self flashes its reaction into a mind that is unable to interpret and sort out the messages of the real self from those that come from the child within.

The fact that the other does not fulfill our needs also weakens our conviction that we have a right to the pleasure we so much desire. We vaguely suspect that we may be wrong to even want this pleasure. Thus we begin to displace the original, natural need and desire for pleasure into other channels where they are sublimated. Other, more or less compulsive needs come into existence. All the while we are torn between the force of the deeply hidden original need and the doubt that we have a right to its fulfillment. The more we doubt, the more dependent we become on reconfirmation by an outside authority — a parent-substitute, public opinion or organization that represents the last word or truth to us.

The more this vicious cycle goes on, the less pleasure remains in the psyche, while displeasure accumulates. Such a person must increasingly despair about life and doubt that fulfillment is possible. There comes a point when a person inwardly gives up.

Every one of us is affected by this problem at least to some degree. There is a place inside of us that is fearful and weak. In this secret corner we feel not only helpless and dependent but also deeply ashamed. The shame is due to the method we employ to placate the person who at any given period is supposed to fulfill the role of authority and grant us what we need in way of pleasure, safety and self-respect.

So when two such people get together to some degree or another there is a level of co-dependency. They each come together and depend on each other for their feelings of love, pleasure, safety and self-respect. They approach each other from "you must" and they each make demands to be, feel, and do what each needs and desires.

These demands on each other may not be manifested outwardly or assertively at all. In fact, on the surface such a person may totally lack self-assertion. Our inability or difficulty to healthily assert ourselves is a direct result of having to hide the underlying, shameful and threatening vicious cycle. It is threatening because we know quite well that if it shows openly, it will evoke great censure and disapproval and possibly overt rejection.

To actualize our authentic power and our full human potential we must vigorously face this area within ourselves. All of us must tackle it, if we wish to realize life and our own best potential and if we wish to discover our own infinite powers to create infinite goodness in our lives.

The stronger the "you must" is secretly thrown at others, the more we inactivate our own powers. As a result of that we become paralyzed, inactive in body, heart, soul and mind. This inactivity keeps us from moving into our own center, the place where all realistic promise and all potential for every kind of fulfillment and delight exist. We inadvertently make ourselves hang unto others, which must elicit hate in us. Finding the treasures of our own center makes us free. Then, contact with others becomes a delightful intrigue and luxury that elicits love.

When we continually use inner, covert pressure on others because we believe that we are dependent on them, we diminish our own power and energy supply. If our energy is used in its natural, correct, and meaningful way, it never exhausts itself. Our energy only exhausts itself when it is wrongly used. There are innumerable methods, which we use in order to switch on this forcing-current. They include: compliance in varying degrees, passive resistance, spite, withdrawal, refusal to co-operate, forceful outer aggression, intimidation, and persuasion through false strength and assumption of an authority role. Deep down they all mean "you must love me and give me what I need". The more blindly we are involved in this way of being, the more we weaken and further alienate ourselves from the center of our true inner life, where we find all that we can ever need and want.

Let Go

In order to get over our dependency and actualize our full human potential, the following has to happen: we must forgive and let go of the particular person or persons from whom we expect our life fulfillment and whom we simultaneously resent for that very fact. We must all recognize that we place expectations and make demands on others that no one but ourselves can fulfill. All we need and long for, including real love, can only come when our soul is fearless and we know that the strength of our feelings with which we can give and receive love is located within us. For as long as we hang on to another person in the way of a child denying the adult we are, we enslave ourselves in the true sense of the word. The more we do this the less we can either receive or give and the less any real feeling of any sort about any vital experiences can find their home within.

We must learn to let out our negative emotions in a way that does not harm anyone. We must let out our fear, guilt, grief and anger. Letting out fear, guilt, grief and anger makes room for the good feelings. So many of us are still locked and paralyzed. Expressing fear, guilt, grief and anger is the last thing we want to do. Even if we admit to such negative emotions in principle, we still prefer to act them out in unconscious ways, rather than expressing them directly and taking responsibility for them. We still claim a false perfection, even though we do not really believe that they exist in us any longer, in order to favorably dispose others towards us. Some of us even cling for dear life to negative emotions because we fear positive feelings. This is yet another aspect of the same vicious cycle.

The less we see ourselves as responsible for the negative feelings we still possess as well as for our right and ability to create happiness, the more we live in fear. Consequently, the more we must do something to eliminate that fear. Thus negative motivation comes about. We live a makeshift life of avoidance rather than creating an expansive and unfolding life, filled with positive experiences and pleasure.

We must be willing to let go of all negatives in our lives. This can not be forced upon one who has not recognized the dependency in the first place. But once you recognize it, it becomes possible to give up what one has been tightly holding on to. This loosening up must occur to bring about a change in the balance structure of soul force, so those benign cycles can begin to perpetuate themselves.

What we desire in principle may be good and within our right. But when used in a hidden emotional vicious cycle we go about seeking satisfaction in the wrong way and not granting the other person the same freedom we wish for ourselves. We do not give the other person the right to freely choose who to love and accept, and the right not to be rejected and hated for asserting this freedom. We do not even give the other the right to be wrong without being hated and totally denied. This is a freedom, which we much wish for ourselves, and we deeply resent when others do not grant it to us.

In order to liberate our authentic self we must find an area of our life where we are most bound and anxious. Ask yourselves what is it that you want from the other that you are so bounded, so resentful, so afraid, so weak, and so unable to be or do for yourself. This leash can be given up only when we stop wanting from others what we must provide for ourselves. We must verbalize concisely to ourselves whatever we find we need from others; this will bring us nearer to letting go. We will then know that this is the decisive, compulsive need with which we enslave, weaken and paralyze ourselves.

When we let go, we will experience new, resilient strength coming out of us that suddenly conciliate apparently in solvable problems. We will become free as we let go and let free. Only when we can lose on the ego level can we win on the level of the authentic and higher self.

Conversely, our inability to let go, to be fair, to let others be free, our desire to always win and to have our way over others, and our refusal to lose on the ego-level, makes it impossible for us to win on the level of the higher self, where it matters most and where we will find our real strength. Jesus meant this when he said, "he who wants to live must be willing to lose his life." If we insist that we must win on the ego-level, we cannot truly win on the soul level. If we can lose on that ego-level we will surely win on the higher level. We will then inevitably come into that center of ourselves, where our authentic power exists.

As we grant others the right to be, whether it is convenient to us or not, to that extent we will truly find our own right. It is a steady and continuing growing process to find these rights. The process will first manifest by our desire to no longer sell out or degrade ourselves. We will find good defenses against abuse and we will feel good about ourselves. Later we will discover our ever- increasing right for pleasure and happiness. We will find that we move towards a vision of what our life will be. Towards possibilities we never dreamt could exist. We will suddenly permit ourselves pleasure. We will no longer cramp up against it, as we inadvertently continue to do now. We will stop undermining the spontaneous processes, and will learn to trust them. This will open a richness of life and a security that truly are heavenly. By letting go and giving up our inner forcing-current we will experience the beauty of free, unforced and authentic relationships.

When we live in the old dependency pattern we force others to make them do what we want. Thus we create mutual forcing-currents. This weakens us and creates a host of negative emotions that cause us to lose contact with our higher selves, our center, our real being as well as with our good feeling and authentic power.

When we allow our ego to lose gracefully, we will find a treasure within, a new way of life that is an entirely new venture on which we are just embarking. Our fear and tension will dissolve. The inner child will cease to exist and give way to the higher self.

The Higher Self

When we are caught in our vicious cycle, our personality is an instrument of our inner child and our ego. There is no contact with our authentic power and our higher self. Once we have successfully dealt with our inner child, we break free of our vicious cycle and can then contact and live as our higher self.

Most people use the terms "higher self" and "soul" interchangeably. I define higher self as the self that knows and carries out the goals of our soul. When our personality is fully developed, integrated, and evolved, it becomes an instrument through which our soul can fulfill its goals. It becomes more than a personality; it evolves into our higher self. However, the fusion of our mind, emotions and body – being your higher self – is different from being our soul. Our higher self is a perfect instrument through which our soul can express itself on the earth plane. As our higher self, we carry out the purpose of our soul, instead of following the desires of our personality. We are being our higher selves every time we align our personality with our soul and carry out our soul's goals.

Instead of living as our higher self, most of us live as our inner child. The personality must overcome the cravings of the inner child, so it can grow into the higher self, thus being able to contact the soul and live the soul's purpose. In order to experience authentic power and our full human potential we must overcome our inner child and live as our higher selves.

We must reach into our inner being and communicate with it for the purpose of eliminating these weaknesses in us that bind us back in our life. No matter how much we may justify this holding back it serves no good purpose. Mankind has held back for millions of years saying that pleasure is wrong, frivolous and unspiritual. Yet we cannot come face to face with our authentic power until we first come face to face with our weakness and dependency. Only by facing this aspect of our being can we face our strengths and beauty and all the potential that exists in us in a way that we cannot as yet fathom.

CHAPTER 15

OVERCOMING OUR FEARS

We've got to be taught to hate and fear...
It's got to be drummed in our dear little ear.

Fear is the greatest immobilizer to happiness, effectiveness, achievement, enjoyment and authentic power. Fear retards our progress and causes inaction when action is what is needed the most. Fear is not something we were born with; it is something that was drummed into our heads. Fear in one form or another is the number one reason why most of us do not complete what we are here to accomplish. In order for us to experience true success and real freedom we must learn how to deprogram and conquer our fears.

The two main ways in which fear was initially learned was from our care-givers — our parents, teachers, society — and from our early experiences associated with some kind of physical or emotional pain or hurt. Therefore, some type of hurt is at the foundation of all fear. Fear is a reactive mechanism to avoid hurt – physical, mental or emotional. There is the story of a cat that once jumped on a hot stove and burnt itself – that cat never jumped on a stove again, hot or cold. That cat developed a reactive mechanism for avoiding being hurt by the stove. Many human beings behave in the same way.

Parentally Instilled Fear

Your parents must have said to you, as mine did, "don't run out in the street — you will get killed by a car." Taken literally that statement is of course not necessarily true. All of us walk out into the street and don't usually get hit by a car. Our parents thought that part of their loving mission was to instill fear in order to protect us, so that we would think before darting out into the street to chase a ball. Unfortunately, the more our parents repeated fear- instilling statements, the more they became programmed into our subconscious minds as a reality.

What our parents and caregivers meant to instill, was a sense of caution. They meant to say "when approaching a street be careful and cautious, look both ways before crossing, so that you don't attempt to occupy the same space at the same time as an automobile, because the result may not be favorable to you." Our parents meant to teach us caution as well as common sense, but instead they inadvertently instilled fear into us.

Fear of Pain

The second way fear is programmed into our minds is as a result of experiences we don't quite understand and which cause us some kind of emotional or physical pain. For example, if a child grabs a hot pot on a heated stove, he or she will immediately jerk his or her hand away. No thinking required. However, that event may cause that child to become unnecessarily afraid of fire, or anything that appears hot. No real danger is inherent in the fire or the hot pot, but only in the way you interact with them. It is natural to be cautious with things that are hot and could injure you if you touch them, but it is unnatural to be afraid of them.

Our bodies were made in such a way as to feel pain to alert us that something was not right in our environment and we should check it out before it destroys us. Pain and physical hurt operate like the oil light in our car, which tells us when the oil is low and that it is time to take action. Pain therefore is not something we should fear, but something we should understand and use to protect our bodies.

The experience of pain is one of the strongest causes of fear. The pain is remembered, the memory causes habitual thoughts and actions, and these habits dominate how we live our lives. When fear causes us to form behavior patterns, those patterns become walls, and we live our lives as if trapped and powerless. We live our lives as a plant in a flowerpot. If the plant were in the forest, it would eventually fill the forest with the beauty and fragrance of a million flowers. If fear motivates your life, you will live like a flower in a small pot, with a few other flowers stuck into the soil beside you to make you seem alive.

The depth of fear programmed in our minds is controlled by two elements: firstly, the depth of emotion you experience during or after any single traumatic event and secondly, the number of repetitions of fear-producing experiences.

When we experience a traumatic event causing us physical pain such as being bitten by a dog, bee, or an emotional pain, such as a loss of love or a psychological situation, such as, being embarrassed after a public speaking engagement, we store these events in our subconscious mind as hurt and fear. The depth of the fear is a function of the depth of the emotion we first felt. And if these fear-producing events are repeated, our fear of those events intensifies.

When we say that we are afraid of something, what we are really saying is that we don't like the intense emotions we experience when confronted by that thing. The emotions are not dangerous, only unpleasant or negative. Yet we begin to avoid more and more of those experiences, even opportunities, in order not to trigger those emotions.

Events, circumstances and situations have no real fear associated with them. Yet because of the fear programmed in our minds, confronting these circumstances causes our survival system to react. Our survival system brings back the exact feeling as the first time we experienced the first event. For example, if a big white dog bit a child — that child is very likely to go through his or her life being afraid of big white dogs. Moreover, every time that child sees a big white dog, not only will he or she remember the bite, but will also experience the same feeling and emotion as the first time the encounter occurred.

Remember when you were naturally fearless, doing things you wouldn't even dream of doing now? As you get older, you become more and more fearful, and each fear becomes self-perpetuating. The process can and must be deprogrammed and reversed if you are to be self- actualized and achieve your highest and best. Otherwise, your life will be lived in a box that will continually become smaller and smaller. From the time you were born until now, you have subconsciously taken on dozens of fears, some of which have severe negative reactions and consequences. These fears act as obstacles and stumbling blocks toward the road of self-expression, self-fulfillment and self-actualization.

Fear Causes Inaction and Avoidance

Fear is dangerous to your health, wealth, and happiness, as well as your peace of mind. We were taught that fear is healthy and natural, because it cautions us about potentially dangerous situations. It is not! Fear is unhealthy and unnatural, and we must get rid of the impact that fear has on us. Achieving our purpose and operating at maximum effectiveness depends on it. Fears are the fundamental building blocks of the brick wall between you and your destination. To achieve our full human potential, there is no doubt that we must continually face the very things that we fear the most. The alternative is to give up on your dreams and vision and settle for mediocrity.

The movie "The Last Temptation of Christ" showed the

possibility of Jesus Christ not living his vision. The result was the way most of us live our lives — a pathetic existence in which our spirits and soul long depart the body, and what's left is a zombie. In the end, one will conclude that it is much more desirable for you to just face your fears and accomplish your mission.

If we are to accomplish what we are here for, we will have to be confident and vigilant, we will have to be trail blazers, constantly sailing uncharted waters, doing things we have never done before and some things that have never been done by anyone before. This kind of life calls forth the best within us and a daily routine of facing greater and greater challenges and fears. Once we conquer one, we move on to a greater one until we accomplish our purpose here. This is the only type of life worth living. Until we face and challenge our fears, they enslave us.

We must make it a priority to deprogram the fears that are causing continuous ineffectiveness in our lives. I will suggest strategies that you can use to squelch your ingrained fears and transform you into a fearless person, full of determination and courage.

Constantly Confront the Things You Fear

Our fears limit our enjoyment of life, our ability to achieve our purpose and our effectiveness in achieving our goals. For example, if you are afraid of drowning, you may choose not to learn to swim. One of the best ways to deprogram and get over your fears is to face them head on. The experience of conquering your fears is freeing and such a confidence builder, that every fear-busting experience is worth it. When we find the courage to go through the thing we fear, we emerge on the other side a much freer and more powerful person.

We must come to the realization that that which we fear

controls us and what we trust or control has no power over our lives. Conquering fear can be an exciting experience when it is accomplished in a spirit of challenge and fun. To make that kind of excitement part of your own experience, include on a list of goals all that you desire to conquer, including your fears.

The total lack of fear is the fundamental mechanism that opens the door to your magnificence and authenticity. Fearlessness will bring you happiness, richness and success in your personal, business and spiritual life. People are reluctant to challenge a fearless person because that is a person who cannot be upset, intimidated, or manipulated. A fearless person is like a warship sailing through an ocean filled with small fish — unstoppable. Supreme self-confidence comes from knowing that you are totally capable of handling anything that comes up in your life. It is the true experience of your authentic self.

ACT EVEN IN THE FACE OF FEAR

We were taught that a good excuse is acceptable when we did not have the result we set out to accomplish. This is not true. We either have the results or we have nothing – excuses don't count. Fear is one of the excuses we use for not having the result. If we live our lives by avoiding our fears, we will never achieve anything worthwhile. Opportunities will slip by unnoticed. Great potential experiences will be lost, and life will become mundane and boring instead of magnificent and effervescent.

If we were totally fearless, we would master all of our challenges in this lifetime. We have the choice of facing our fears, and getting beyond them. We must realize that it is okay to be afraid and still act. To successfully conquer fear we must be committed to act, even in the face of fear.

CREATE A MIND MOVIE OF THE EVENT YOU FEAR

A second method of deprogramming fear, is to confront what you fear in your mind, instead of in your environment. Your fears are in your mind, so you can use your mind to deprogram them, by using what is called a mind movie — the experience of a real event that occurs in your imagination only. Mind movies are an extremely effective fear-busting technique and are at least half as effective and much less costly and time consuming in deprogramming fears as facing the actual fear-triggering event. To create a mind movie, find a quiet place to sit, relax your entire body, close your eyes and envision yourself going through the fear-triggering situation over and over in your mind. See yourself handling and conquering the situation effectively and successfully. See yourself as the victor, the winner, and you will find the fear getting less ominous. This positive programming will override the negative programming in your mind and significantly reduce your fears.

Subconsciously, we generally avoid what we fear, as well as any environment in which the fear might be triggered. By consciously or subconsciously avoiding all situations, events and circumstances that our fears may trigger, we set limits for all our experiences. Limited potential experiences inhibit our alternatives and build unscaleable walls around our opportunities. If we are willing to accept the challenge of facing what we fear, we will find that our fears will back down. We can expand the limits of our experiences, to the point where nothing in life — not things, events, situations, circumstances, or people — can hold us back or render us ineffective.

FEAR OF TRUTH

Our most significant fears have a deeper origin and more ominous beginnings than just pain and the development of thought. When a decision is required, there is a tendency to make the wrong decision more often than mere chance would suggest. If we could reach into our mind, we could see what we are doing. There is a part of our being that always knows the truth. We can witness the fact that when we perceive the truth, there is a fear and denial of that truth. This fear and denial is where our ego begins.

We react with fear many times when we have a subtle recognition of truth that we don't want to acknowledge. We deny the truth and run from it. Then we react and attack. We submerge the truth with the sound of thought, and in a flash our brain has vanquished the light of truth. This is one of the ways we develop our subconscious minds. We have an awareness of some truth, and immediately there is fear and we deny that truth.

We are afraid of our magnificence. Deep down we know that we are special beings, who came here for a special purpose. Each time we get an insight as to who we really are or why we are here, we cringe and run into hiding. We will do anything to hide from the extraordinary beings that we are — sometimes even commit suicide — because we are afraid of the power that we are. I like the now popular quote from Nelson Mandela's presidential inaugural speech that states

> "Our worst fear is not that we are inadequate,
> our deepest fear is that we are powerful beyond
> measure. It is our light, not our darkness that most
> frightens us. We ask ourselves, "Who am I to be
> brilliant, gorgeous, talented and fabulous?"
> Actually, who are you not to be? You are a child of
> God; your playing small doesn't serve the world.
> There is nothing enlightened about shrinking so
> that other people won't feel insecure around you.
> We were born to make manifest the glory of God
> within us. It is not just in some of us, it is in

everyone and as we let our own light shine we unconsciously give other people permission to do the same. As we are liberated from our own fear our presence automatically liberates others."

Fear vs. Love

The root of all negative emotions, such as hate, jealousy, resentment and guilt, is fear. The root of all positive emotions, such as forgiveness, trust and happiness, is love. Love and trust are the opposition of fear. The most powerful way to overcome fear is to replace fear with love. Know that whatever you are experiencing, you brought into your life, consciously or subconsciously, to teach you a lesson. If you relax and go through the experience with love and positive emotion, instead of fear and negative emotion, you would have learned a valuable lesson and made a step forward on the road towards achieving your full human potential.

CHAPTER 16

INTERDEPENDENCE

Toward an authentic community consciousness

Throughout this book we have been looking at strategies and tools to empower our lives. Some may think that personal power negates the need for community. This is not so at all. In fact authentic power is community power. The two are interrelated and indispensable to each other. Authentic power seeks to develop and serve the community. Fundamentally we are here to serve one another. Living a life of authentic power is all about serving humanity.

Interdependence and genuine community are not very popular in our present society. We have been inculcated in a paradigm of individuality. Many of us believe that to succeed, means that we have to be independent, ruthless and fiercely competitive. We are also taught that the world is a cruel place and that one cannot trust another, sometimes not even one's closest relatives and friends. "I am on my own. I am alone. I am independent!" seems to be the cry of modern man and woman.

To a degree, our independence is unavoidable, inescapable and even desirable. We all recognize the process into adulthood. We say to our self "I have to grow up; I have to leave my parents' care and stand on my own". Indeed this process towards independence is vital for our overall development and maturity. To become a functional adult, we have to realize our uniqueness and strive to empower and develop ourselves to the best of our abilities. All of us are called to individual power, development and independence. In this developmental process, we must learn to take full responsibility for ourselves. Indeed, this process is crucial for our physical, emotional, mental and spiritual growth and development, and should not be compromised. For we need to develop a sense of autonomy and self-determination. We must seek to become captains of our own ships and masters of our destiny.

However, our individualism and independence are only parts of our nature. To be whole and complete, we need to be interdependent as well. We can never be whole and completely in and of ourselves. We cannot be all things to ourselves and to others at all times, and that's why the principle of interdependence and community is so important. We cannot be mother, father, doctor, carpenter, lawyer, teacher, farmer and engineer, all rolled into one at all times. While it is true that we are all created unique and are challenged to power and independence, the reality is that there is a point beyond which our sense of self-determination and independence not only becomes narcissistic and prideful, but increasingly self-defeating and community defeating.

Fundamentally, we are inevitably social creatures, who desperately need each other for healing, sustenance and wholeness. We need to be involved in community, not just for our survival, but to give meaning to life. This realization is the paradoxical root, from which authentic community can grow and flourish.

On the one hand, we are called to individual wholeness, and simultaneously to recognition of our incompleteness; called to power and to acknowledge our weakness when we stand alone. Thus, the principle of community is the recognition that we are called to both independence and interdependence.

The problem with most of the modern schools of

thought is that they explore only one side of the puzzle, embracing only one half of our humanity. They recognize that we are called to individual power, independence, and individual wholeness. But they deny entirely the other side of the human story; that we can never fully get to our completeness on our own, that we are in our uniqueness weak, and imperfect (NB is this a contradiction with being perfect as we are?) creatures who need each other's love, empathy and healing, along our spiritual journey.

This denial of the fact that we need each other can only be sustained by pretence and hiding behind masks, because we can never be totally adequate, and totally self-sufficient, beings. The ideal archetype of individualism encourages us to fake it. The cliché for this way of thinking is to, "fake it till you make it". The unfortunate thing is that we cannot make it alone and so we end up living a life of perpetual lies and pretence. This paradigm of total independence and individualism encourages us to hide our weaknesses, and the fact that we need each other's closeness and love. It teaches us to be ashamed of our limitations.

This paradigm of rugged individualism drives us to wear mask after mask to cover any perceived weaknesses. It forces us to constantly appear as if we are in control. It demands that we keep up the facade and isolate ourselves from each other. We are afraid to allow anyone to discover that we are not what we pretend to be. In this game, no one has any access to our authenticity. This air of pretentiousness makes the development of authentic and genuine community almost impossible.

This method of existence leads to a life of sadness and loneliness. We are so lonely we cannot even acknowledge our loneliness to ourselves, much less to others. We just have to look at the sad, frozen faces all around us each day, filled with frustration, fear, anger and guilt. We could search in vain for the souls hidden behind the masks of pretentious composure and the "looking good". Life should not be this way, yet most of us do not know an alternative way to be.

I am reminded of an anonymous poem I read a long time ago, which depicts very clearly the results of living the life of individualism filled with masks, pretences and loneliness. I have reproduced it below in its entirety.

> "Don't be fooled by me. For I wear a mask. I wear a thousand masks. Masks that I'm afraid to take off, and none of them are mine. Pretending is an art that's second nature with me, but don't be fooled, for God's sake, don't be fooled.
>
> I give you the impression that I'm secure, that all is sunny, and coolness is my game; that the water's calm, I'm in command, and that I need no one. But don't believe me...Please don't! My surface may seem smooth, but my surface is my mask... My ever varying and ever concealing mask. Beneath swells the real me, in confusion, in fear and in aloneness. But I hide this; I don't want anybody to know it.
>
> I panic at the thought of my weakness, and the fear of being exposed. That's why I frantically create a mask to hide behind... a nonchalant, sophisticated facade... to help me pretend, to shield me from your glance... a glance that "knows." But, such a glance is precisely my salvation... My only salvation... and I know it! But, provided that glance is followed by acceptance, and then followed by love. It's the only thing that will assure me of what I can't assure myself... that I'm really "worth" something.
> But, I don't tell you this. I don't dare. I'm afraid to. I'm afraid you will think less of me, that you'll laugh, and your laugh would kill me. I'm afraid that deep down I'm "nothing," that I'm just no good, and that

you will see this and reject me.

So I play my game, my desperate, pretending game, with a facade of assurance on the outside, and a trembling child within. And, so begins the parade of masks, the glittering, but empty parade of masks, and my life becomes a front. I idly chatter to you in the suave tones of surface talk. I tell you everything that's really nothing, and nothing of that which is everything... of what's crying within me.
So, when I'm going through my routine, do not be fooled by what I'm saying. Please listen carefully, and try to hear what I'm "not" saying... what I'd like to be able to say, what, for survival, I need to say, but can't say. I dislike hiding... honestly, I do. I dislike the superficial game I'm playing... the superficial, phony game. I'd really like to be genuine and spontaneous, and "me." Help me!

You've got to hold out your hand... even when that's the last thing I seem to want or need. Only you can wipe away from my eyes the blank stare of the breathing dead. Each time you try to understand, because you really care, my heart begins to grow wings... very small wings, very feeble wings... but wings.

With your sensitivity, sympathy, and your power of understanding, you can breathe life into me. I want you to know that. I want you to know how important you are to me. How you can be a creator of the person that is me, if you choose to... please choose to.
You alone can break down the wall behind which I tremble. You alone can remove my mask. You alone can release me from my shadow world of panic and uncertainty... from my lonely prison. So do not pass me by. Please don't pass me by!

It will not be easy for you. A long conviction of worthlessness builds strong walls. The nearer you approach me... the blinder I may strike back! It's irrational, but despite what the good books say about man... I am irrational. I fight against the very thing that I cry out for.

But, I am told that love is stronger than strong walls, and in this lies my hope... my only hope. Please try to beat down those walls with firm hands, but with gentle hands... for a child is very sensitive, and I am a child.

Who am I, you may wonder? I am someone you know very well.

For I am every man you meet...

And I am every woman you meet...

And I am you!"

We are desperately in need of a new paradigm, which teaches that we cannot truly be ourselves, until we are able to share freely the things we most have in common — our humanity — our love, strength, weaknesses, inadequacies, successes and failures.

This new paradigm of wholeness will allow those necessary barriers, or outlines, of our individual selves to be like permeable membranes, permitting our authentic selves to seep out and the authentic selves of others to seep in. It is a paradigm of living that acknowledges our interdependence, not merely in the intellectual domain but in the depths of our hearts as well. It is this paradigm of reality that makes authentic community possible.

THE TRUE MEANING OF COMMUNITY

The word "community" is used very loosely in everyday language. We use community to refer to almost any group of people who come together on a regular basis, but is that really community? Is that the type of community that I am talking about here? For example, does a family, church, school, town, company, organization necessarily constitute a community? We normally apply the term "community" to almost any group, regardless of how poorly they communicate. Well, this is not what I am talking about in the new paradigm of community.

When I use the word "community", I am referring to groups of individuals who have learnt how to communicate honestly and openly with each other — a group of persons whose relationship goes deeper than their masks of composure, and who have developed some significant commitment to each other. This can take place in a family, a church, an organization, a company or an association.

There is a special power to community, which is much greater than the combined power of the individuals involved. This community power is something that has not yet been fully explained or understood. There is something about the power of community, which is inherently mysterious and unfathomable. Authentic community is always "something" more than the sum of the individuals in it. It is this "something else", that is capable of transforming our lives and our world, through community.

One of the most fundamental components of community is commitment. Most of us are so fickle, that at the slightest evidence of confusion, we go packing. The process of coming into community is not usually an easy one. It takes time, effort and commitment. Commitment to community is the ability to totally accept others and the willingness to co-exist. For the development of community, the members sooner or later must commit themselves to one another, if they are to become or stay in community. Entering into community is like entering into a marriage and requires that we hang in there, when the going gets a little rough. Community formation and maintenance requires a high degree of commitment.

Before a group can solidify into community, the individuals must learn to transcend individual differences. Differences are appreciated, celebrated and welcomed instead of being ignored, denied, hidden or changed. The individuals must learn to unconditionally accept themselves and each other. It is not just tolerance for each other but unconditional acceptance. Only at this stage of development can a group of individuals experience the benefit and joy of being part of an authentic community.

While the paradigm of independence predisposes one to arrogance, the paradigm of community leads to humility. We begin to appreciate each other's gifts and each individual in the group begins to recognize and appreciate their own limitations. When we witness others share their brokenness, we become more able to accept our own inadequacy and imperfections. As we become more aware of our selves and of others, we will begin to recognize and appreciate the interdependence of all humanity. As we become a community — we become more and more humble and more and more human — not only as individuals but also as a group.

Community Consciousness

Authentic community must be self-aware and self-conscious. It must examine itself. It must know itself. In order for a group to know itself, it must notice, observe, contemplate and inquire into itself. The essential goal of this contemplation and inquiry is increased awareness of the world inside and outside oneself and the relationship between them. A person who settles for a relatively limited awareness of him or herself is not psychologically, mentally, emotionally and spiritually mature. Self- examination is the key to insight, which is the key to wisdom. Plato said; "The life which is unexamined is not worth living".

Like an individual, a community must become conscious of itself and contemplate its existence. Likewise, a community that settles for relatively limited awareness of itself is psychologically, emotionally and spiritually immature.

A community that is unconscious of itself and its' reason for existence, will not be able to set and accomplish worthy goals. A community without a vision and a purpose will perish and dissipate.

COMMUNITY VISION AND PURPOSE

The simple most important activity for members of a community to focus on is defining their vision and purpose for being together. In much the same way as a person's individual purpose creates the inspiration for his or her life, the community purpose creates the inspiration for the life of the community. When there is a clear alignment in purpose among the participants, each moves forward in the activities of the group with total confidence, congruency and alignment. It is crucial to define a community purpose and clarify each member's alignment,with the group for maximum achievement.

One of the problems with group purpose is that it is handed down from a leader or an executive committee. Most of the members do not feel that the purpose adequately reflects their reason for joining, or feel alienated from the process. A simple method that I use when working on developing group purpose, is for each member of the community (if a very large community, then I divide it up into small groups) to separately define his or her purpose for the group. Then the participants share their purpose with each other. The next step is for the group to create a single statement of community purpose.

Nothing is more important to a group, community or organization than having a clearly defined purpose or vision, which inspires every member of the group. The creation of such a group purpose assures the success of the group. This can be reduced to a mission statement, which captures the essence of the community vision and purpose in a simple short statement. It is best when the entire group helps in the creation of this statement.

Unconditional Love

Unconditional love forms a key precept in the interdependence paradigm. Love involves accepting all people and all things as they are, even while working toward positive change. Community is a safe place because each member is accepted just the way that he or she is. Members are free to be themselves. It is essential for each member to express unconditional love and support for each other. Unconditional love and support means seeing persons as perfect just the way they are. Loving unconditionally means recognizing that if another person's behavior offends us, that behavior represents a part of ourselves, which we are not willing to accept and love just the way it is.

We must be careful however, not to confuse unconditional love with the need to do anything outwardly. Unconditional love is something to be, not something to do. It is not an obligation to give money, spend time with someone, or do anything in particular, although it can result in an outward action. In order for it to be beneficial to both parties it must be authentic, voluntary and not from a sense of obligation.

Openness and Vulnerability

Almost every time that I lead a course on paradigm shifting or community development, there is sure to be an occasion when I cry. At those times I notice myself trying to fight back the tears. Having been inculcated in independence and individualism for so long, I still have this urge not to appear vulnerable especially in public. The facade of individualism forces us into looking good all the time. Vulnerability would spoil our "coolness". The paradox is that there is no genuine power without openness and vulnerability.

Once genuine community is achieved, there is an overwhelming feeling of safety. This feeling of safety is a rare and beautiful feeling. Participants feel free to hug and love each other, unconditionally. For the very first time some of us have broken out of our masks and have allowed others to see who we really are, and also to see others for whom they truly are — a magnificent part of God!

This stage of community is not easily achieved. It takes a lot of work for a group of strangers to achieve the safety of true community. Once they succeed however, it is as if the well has broken. As soon as the participants realize that it is safe to share their hearts and that they will be listened to with love, compassion and empathy — they become overjoyed to release years, sometimes decades, of pent-up frustration, hurt, anger, resentment and guilt. One person's sharing provides the space for another person's sharing and so it snowballs.

Once members in the group start sharing and find themselves being loved, valued and appreciated, they become more and more open. The mask, walls and pretences come tumbling down. As they tumble, as the love and acceptance escalates, as the mutual intimacy multiplies, true healing takes place. Old wounds are healed, old resentments are forgiven, old resistances are conquered, and fear is replaced by trust.

Trust

Trust is one of the most salient principles in the formation and maintenance of community. It is also the principle with which most of us struggle the most. In our contemplation we must ask ourselves some searching questions about our relationship with trust. Questions such as: Who do I trust?

Who don't I trust? Why do I trust some people? Why don't I trust other people? Where did my relationship with trust come from?

A trusting state is one of the most fundamental states toward creating authentic and genuine community. Lack of trust causes severe scarcities of genuine community in our world.

A major part of our relationship with trust is that we don't trust ourselves. We believe that we are not good enough; not worthy. Each of us is born knowing everything we need to know. It is programmed in our genes. It is connected to our mission and purpose in life. We are genetically coded for genius. When we realize this, we not only learn to trust ourselves but we simultaneously learn to trust each other.

When offered the opportunity of a safe place, most people will naturally begin to experiment more deeply than ever before with love, trust, acceptance and forgiveness. We drop our customary defenses, threatened postures, and the barriers of distrust, fear, resentment and prejudice. When we are safe, there is a natural tendency for us to heal ourselves. We have within us a natural yearning and thrust towards health and wholeness. Most of the time, however, this thrust, this energy, is enchained by fear and neutralized by defenses and resistance. When we are in a safe place, where these defenses and resistance are no longer necessary, then the thrust towards health is liberated.

Genuine acceptance and trust must start with self. If we are not able to trust, love, accept and forgive ourselves, we will be unable to extend that to others. Most of us think that we have to have reasons to love ourselves. But, we must learn to love ourselves unconditionally, just the way we are, right where we are. We must practice loving ourselves.

> I forgive myself
> I trust myself

I love myself &
I accept myself

Once we have mastered the art of forgiving, loving trusting, and accepting ourselves, we are then and only then, in a position to extend that love to others.

I forgive you
I trust you
I love you
I accept you

Once we are willing to both grant love to ourselves and to send love to another – only then do we open the door to receive.

I accept your forgiveness
I receive your Trust
I receive your acceptance
I accept your love

Trust Cycle
I trust myself so much
That I can trust you so much
That you can trust you so much
That you can trust me

We have evolved to this point in our existence on this planet by default. We have a powerful opportunity to move into the next millenium by design. To make this evolutionary step forward we need personal power and we need each other.

PART V

THE SPIRITUAL

The Nature of Existence
The Nature of the Soul
The Nature of God

CHAPTER 17

THE NATURE OF EXISTENCE

The basic level of the universe is consciousness — pure intelligence. At the quantum level the universe is simply energy and information. It is an information processor — like a mind.

As a species we have been pondering the nature of life and existence for millenniums. Understanding the nature and the working of the universe are keys to understanding the nature of existence and who we are as human beings. This understanding will greatly assist us on our journey to authentic power.

This universe can be divided into three fundamental planes or levels of existence – spirit, mind and body. Spirit is the first and the highest plane. Within that plane dwell different levels as well, the highest is the One, the indescribable and unfathomable — usually referred to as God, Universal Energy, Universal Mind, Universal Principle or the Law. This is the highest and the ultimate realm of all spiritual and mystical traditions, where space and time and words have no meaning. It is the highest point of spiritual evolution. This is the goal of all intelligent life in the universe. Our quest is to evolve through the other planes of existence to unite and commune with this highest level.

The second level of existence is the mind. It connects the spiritual realm to the physical realm. This is the basic current of the universe. At this level of the universe, the idea of space and time does not exist. At this level it is not possible to locate the specific position and speed of an electron. It has no specific location. Scientists in our world have not located it as yet and are calling it quantum space. Scientists have not been able to locate consciousness in the brain either. In fact they have no idea where consciousness is located in the human being. That is because it is like the basic quantum level of the universe.

The basic level of the universe is consciousness – pure intelligence. At the quantum level the universe is simply energy and information. It is an information processor – like a mind. The informational flows around and through all biological processes. All things are intimately and infinitely connected by the flow of the consciousness. Nature is purposive and it possesses deep intentionally. The laws that govern the universe are contained at this quantum – mind – level. The human being who is capable of deep inner reflection will gain the secrets of the universe, because that is where they are kept.

The third and lowest plane of existence is the physical world. This is the level of consciousness in which we feel ourselves existing as a human body in a physical world and feel ourselves separated from universal energy and power.

As a result we experience a place filled with trouble, where we live out our life totally unaware of anything deeper and more profound. The world as it is has nothing wrong but our trouble begins when we deny the power and intelligence that is our essence and hold firmly to the view that all we are is a physical body in a physical world.

Spirit
The Power
The One – God
The Unfathomable

Mind
Universal Power
To
Individual bodies of Light
Body
The Physical World

Fulfillment

The ultimate goal of all intelligent life in the universe is to evolve to the point where it can unite and commune with the One, the Universal Power, the God Energy. In order to do this all intelligent life must grow and master, advance through, the lower planes of existence, before communing with the highest. There is intelligent life at each stage of existence. Beings on a higher plane are consciously aware of beings on a lower plane but not vice versa. Each being exists in its essential state as a soul. Each soul then takes on a different incarnation in which it experiences itself as an ego. The soul chooses a specific life purpose for each incarnation.

Human beings have two main goals. The first is to master the physical world and the second is to realize our highest spiritual fulfillment. The lowest plane of existence is the physical world; our first step on our spiritual evolution is to master the physical world. Once we have mastered the physical plane we can then contact and commune with the highest spiritual power in the universe to begin our spiritual evolution.

When our human life wave was brought into existence, every ego was absolutely ignorant. We knew nothing, but we had certain unique gifts, which were designed to make us learn. Inherent in all egos is mind — a power of the second plane of existence. In this respect we are created in the image of the One. The qualities of mind are memory, desire, will, curiosity, consciousness, conscience, creativity, intuition, emotion and reason. Granted these mental endowments, our task is to learn everything there is to be known about the lowest plane of existence — the physical plane. This involves learning arts, trades and professions, the science of the physical universe, and most importantly, how to get along with other egos socially, intimately, politically, economically and morally.

It is not possible to learn all of this in one lifetime. A soul is allowed many lifetimes to build knowledge and morality into his or her ego's experience. Whatever we are unable to accomplish in one lifetime, we take up in the next until we have mastered our problem. We enter each lifetime with a specific problem to solve, if we don't accomplish that mission we will have to repeat that lifetime until we solve that problem. Step-by-step, life-by- life, we build our soul experience until at last, we master every problem offered by the physical plane of existence.

When we have mastered the physical plane by means of our intellect and have advanced ourselves to the extent that we have fully developed our spiritual bodies, we will then also achieve freedom from re-birth. Forever after we are immortal. We become immortal when we no longer need to occupy a physical body, which is subject to pain, old age, and death. When we earn immortality, we may enjoy continuity of learning upon higher planes without the interruptions inherent in re-birth, childhood, and human error on the physical plane.

We think that people die, but in reality people do not die, only physical bodies die. Humans contain a spirit, and spirit cannot die. The spiritual realm is on a higher plane of existence. We occupy a physical body on the physical plane of existence in order to learn. Our bodies are our vehicles; it provides a means of locomotion and tools in the form of hands and muscles so that we may deal effectively with the world. Once we master the physical plane we no longer need these tools and we need no longer take on a physical body and suffer the limitation of being earth bound. When this stage of freedom from reincarnation is achieved we may then advance more rapidly in understanding of the spiritual plane of existence until we master everything there is to master on both the physical and spiritual planes. When an Ego has added all this knowledge unto himself he is known as a master.

Real Success

Our spiritual fulfillment is to recognize our true spiritual nature, our limitless power and light. We must break through the barrier of fear and contraction that makes this world seem unsatisfactory, and experience once again our limitless spiritual source. We must communicate and commune with the highest spiritual power and transform ourselves into spiritual perfected beings. We must live as enlightened beings in the bliss and the freedom of the highest.

This process can take many lifetimes to attain. Each time a soul descend into the Ego State – it does so with a specific purpose and mission in mind. There is a particular job or experience that will help that soul on its spiritual journey. Each time a soul incarnates however it forgets its connection with the higher plane. It is absorbed into its tribe and is trained to be a "good" tribe member. The typical soul takes on the characteristic of its tribe and forgets all about its mission. The remembering and accomplishment of this mission is what real success is all about.

Energy

Matter and energy cannot be created or destroyed. Energy and matter are manifestation of the same things. Matter can be converted into energy and vice versa. The smallest stand alone component of both matter and energy is an atom. An atom is comprised of a positive center called a nucleus and tiny balls flying around it in orbits (like planets around the sun) called electrons. In actuality none of these subatomic particles are solids. They are bundles of energy. The charges of electricity they are represented to possess are merely a convenience to explain certain attraction and repulsion relative to their charge.

Every particle within an atom moves in an orbit. Even the proton in the atom's nucleus travels a very tight orbit, which determines its apparent diameter. In addition to orbiting there is another important motion of all sub-atomic particles, and this motion is called nutation. Every sub-atomic particle spins about its own internal axis, and nutational refers to a wobble of the axis of rotation.

Each subatomic particle of matter and each quantum-particle of electromagnetic energy spins upon its own axis just the way our planet Earth turns on its poles, and that all these axes wobble at one constant rate regardless of the energy or mass of the particle. It is important to distinguish between spinning and orbiting. Although all particles spin those particles which also travel in closed orbits comprise matter, where as energy particles travel in a straight line. Energy can be converted into matter and vice versa, but the nutational rate of the particles never varies.

Matter is essentially a concept of our sense preceptors which themselves are of the same matter. Our world and everything in it is composed of atoms, but atoms are only packages of energy whose seeming solidity and integrity are due to the circular motions of their components. An atom is almost entirely empty space consisting of a central blob of whirling energy sheathed by the orbits of electrons. The orbiting electrons describe a more-or-less spherical shell of energy; but don't imagine that this shell makes the atom a hollow ball of some concreteness. The emptiness in which the sub-atomic particles exist can be visualized by the supposition that if the nucleus of an atom were enlarged to the size of our sun, then the shell described by its electrons would be twelve times greater than the diameter of our solar system. A pound of lead, which seems quite solid and ponderable to us, is merely an aggregation of swirls of energy separated by comparatively vast reaches of emptiness. This also applies to our bodies. The cells which comprises our tissues, nerves, and blood are of the same intangible swirls.

Therefore everything in the universe is fundamentally energy and information. First energy comes to earth through the radiant light of our sun, stored most directly in green plants, and then distributed throughout the food chain. In the larger sense, we don't just take in energy, we are energy. The organs of our bodies are made of tissues made of cells made of molecules made of atoms made of whirling, pulsating, orbiting, vibrating fields of energy. Energy interpenetrates and comprises the cells of our bodies. We are energy beings made of the same stuffs as the stars.

We know that energy takes many forms, some of which are visible, like a bolt of lightening. Life energy is subtler, we usually cannot see it with our physical eyes, but we can certainly feel it.

There are some scientist working in quantum physics who are making interesting discoveries about the nature of existence. Ever since we opened the door of quantum physic and found that matter is simply energy, scientists have been watching matter turn into energy and energy turn into matter. When studying subatomic particles, it appears that sometimes matter is suddenly created out of nothing, and sometimes disappears back into nothingness. This nothingness that matter seems to come out of and go back into seems very mystical and mysterious. It seems to be playing a primary role at the level of creation and destruction of matter. This is clear evidence of a non-physical foundation to existence.

Quantum physicists have observed that our thoughts

seem to have a very distinct effect on subatomic particles. It seems that we can actually think them into existence. Therefore at the subatomic level we find that the human consciousness has a profound and powerful role to play in the nature of existence. Quantum physics is not only strange to think about, but it is stranger than we can think at this point in our evolution.

Vibration

Reality is not what we see, because everything is vibrating at a different rate of frequency. The difference between a rock, a plant and a person is the difference in the rate of vibration. There is a hierarchy of vibration with matter at the lowest end. Sound is the next level. Some sounds such as radio waves vibrate so fast that we cannot hear them. At higher vibratory rates sound becomes heat, then light. Above that is the level of quantum where mind and consciousness dwell.

All manifestation of thought, emotion, reason, will or desire, or any mental state or condition is accompanied by vibrations. These vibrations are, in a sense, transmitted to the area around them in the same way heat radiates outward from a hot object. Every thought, emotion or mental state has its corresponding rate and mode of vibration. These frequencies can be changed by a change in the thought patterns that inhabit the mind.

Since the universe is also made up of vibration at the deepest and highest level, and the matter and energy that is the universe can be affected and changed just by your attention, the vibrations of the thought that you are thinking may affect the very substance of the universe. The universe will give you what you dwell upon. If you dwell on negativity and fear you will get just that, while if you dwell on positivity and love you will get just that. The universe always answers yes! That is why we have to be very careful what we ask for — for that is exactly what we will get.

Focus on What You Want

Everything in the universe has its opposite. As the Chinese would put it; the yin and the yang. Everything is and isn't at the same time. It is therefore possible to change one mental or emotional state into another. Things belonging to a different class cannot be transformed into each other – however, things of the same class can be transformed into each other. For example, cold cannot be transformed into light, but cold can be transformed into heat, and darkness can be transformed into light.

To change your emotion, simply raise the vibrations of the energy of the emotion and it will be transformed to a higher emotion. In this way, a hateful man can become a loving man by polarizing the emotion along the line of the desired quality. Likewise, to change your mood or your mental state, just change your vibration, through your will power by deliberately fixing your attention on a more desirable state. If you are unhappy deliberately remember times when you were happy. You do not have to get rid of the darkness in the room; just turn on the light and the darkness will disappear.

Cause and Effect

Every thought, emotion, deed or action we engage in, creates results both directly and indirectly. Most people live as if we have nothing to do with the cause side of the "cause and effect equation". Unfortunately we have everything to do with the cause. Yet, most people will die to remain on the effect side of the equation, not at cause, but at effect – at the effect of events, circumstances, situations, other people, the environment. They go about whining and complaining about their powerlessness in the face of nature, events, and other people. They go about giving away their power to affect their futures.

They are riddled with fear, guilt, sorrow, anxiety, self-pity and lack of self-control. This is because they do not understand the law of cause and effect. If they did – they would know that they are the cause of whatever happens to them in this universe. You cannot extend energy and not have it returned to you in like fashion. As you give so shall you receive. By raising your vibratory rate of your thinking you will contact higher energy and will be able to rise above the lower causes and hence the lower effects. The lower causes and effects will therefore not affect you.

The universe is intelligence and conscious. It is therefore possible to affect the fabric of the intelligence that makes up the quantum level of the universe. To achieve the most success we must hold the highest thoughts, emotions and vibratory level.

Infinite Possibilities

Creation is infinite in its possibilities. Our potential for realizing these infinite possibilities of happiness exists in the inner self of each of our beings. Everything in the world exists in a state of potentiality. No person can create anything new. It is impossible for anything new to come into existence; however, it is possible for a person to make manifest something that already exist. It is a fact that everything, absolutely everything exists already on another level of consciousness.

The word "everything", cannot convey the scope of this concept. When one speaks about God's infinity or about creation's infinity this is part of the meaning. There is no state of being, no experience, no situation, no concept, no feeling, and no object that does not already exist. Everything in the world exists in a state of potentiality, which already contains the finished product within it.

This concept is not necessarily easy for most of us to embrace, for it is so contrary to the way we think and experience life in our average level of consciousness. The more we deepen our thoughts on this subject the easier it will become for us to proceed to sense and to grasp it. Knowing and understanding this principle of creation, that all exists already, and that human beings can make these existing impossibilities manifest, is one of the necessary prerequisite in experiencing our authentic power and the fullness of life's infinite potential.

We must first learn how to apply these laws of creation to the problem areas of our life, where we feel troubled, limited or handicapped or trapped. Healthy development and unfoldment of the real self follows the creation of a healthy personality. This can happen once we learn and comprehend that the laws of creation can work only if we apply it first to the troubled areas of our personality. Whatever you can conceive and believe in your mind you can realize. For example, if you are emerged in a conflict in which you cannot conceive of a way out, you truly cannot realize the already existing possibility of a way out. If your concept of a way out is hazy or unrealistic so will the temporary solution appear to you as the only possibility.

This applies to your life on a whole. If you truly comprehend that an infinite number of possibilities exist in any given situation you can find solution even where it was hitherto impossible to do so. It is our responsibility as human beings to make use of these laws of creation and to reach out, so that these infinite possibilities of creation can unfold in enabling us to partake fully of life's offerings.

Therefore, to expand our own possibilities of happiness, we must widen our minds to grasp the principle that we cannot bring something to life, if we cannot first conceive it. We should take some time to ponder this sentence, for understanding this concept will open new doors for us. We should also understand that there is a vast difference between conceiving of further possibilities of expansion or happiness on one hand and day dreaming on the other. Wishful resigned day dreaming that grasps fantasy as a substitute of reality is not at all what is meant here and in fact is a hindrance to the proper perceiving of life's potential.

We need to have vigorous, active and dynamic concepts of what is possible in reality. When we know that something we wish to bring about is possible in principle, you have made the first step towards actualizing it. Most of us conceive of negative possibilities, which we are afraid of and we wish to avoid and defend ourselves against them. Therefore, we are motivated by fear and negative motivation. This is a major obstruction, which encloses us in an imaginary and unnecessary prison. This applies to all levels of our personalities.

This applies to the mental level where we can not really envision the infinite vistas of experiences, of expansion, of stimulation of all sorts of wondrous and happy possibilities that we have a prerogative to achieve in this lifetime. It applies to the emotional level where we do not contain spontaneous and natural flow of our feelings, where we carefully, anxiously and superstitiously hold back. It also applies to the physical level, in that we do not allow our bodies to experience the pleasure it is destined to experience. All these are limitations that we artificially and needlessly picked up on ourselves.

The next obstruction to expanding our life and creating the best that life has in store for us is the misconceptions that are wide spread in the world that we live our lives by. Some of these misconceptions are: "it is not possible to be really great"; "it is not possible to be happy"; "human life is very limited"; "happiness, pleasure and ecstasy are frivolous selfish aims that truly spiritual people forsake for the sake of their spiritual development"; "sacrifice and renunciations are the keys to spiritual development."

We do not have to further elucidate these deeply lodged misconceptions, which are often more unconscious than conscious. But it is necessary for us to discover the subtle ways in which we abide by such general concepts no matter what we consciously believe. We may discover these subtle reactions by observing our reluctance to take steps to realize a perfectly harmless and normal fulfillment of a genuine need or a truly constructive aim. We feel as though something is holding us back, paralyzing our effort. Although there are often a number of other reasons for this reluctance as well.

Fear of happiness, of pleasure, of wide expansion into one's life experiences is based on ignorance that such fulfillment could exist or that you possess all the powers, faculties and resources to create and bring about that you wish. It is also based on misconception that such "pleasure is wrong" or "it is selfish to want personal fulfillment". Fears of happiness are also based on the fear of being annihilated and dissolved, if you ever trusted the flow of the universal force and went with them. Such trust necessitates letting go of the ego-will and the ego-force, and then surrendering to the beneficial force of your deep nature.

CHAPTER 18

THE NATURE OF THE SOUL

Our soul is the truest essence of who we are.

Most of our authentic power lies in our inner being and not our outer. Our outer domain accounts for about five percent of our being. That includes our bodies, emotions and our conscious and subconscious minds. Our soul and our superconscious mind accounts for the other ninety five percent of our being. To live without awareness and active involvement of our inner domain is tantamount to the wealthiest king in the world living as the poorest peasant. It is therefore fundamental that as students of authentic power, we not only understand the nature of the soul, but also how to harmonize our personalities with our souls to achieve wisdom and power.

Our souls are who we are. A personality only exists for a lifetime, but a soul is the composite of all personalities from all lifetimes that we have lived. Stored within our souls are all the experiences gained from our many lives. The soul is responsible for the creation of each personality. It creates the personality for specific reasons to learn or accomplish a specific goal or vision. The soul chooses the particular situations and circumstances in which it will be born and raised. These circumstances are all designed to help the personality learn the tools necessary for it to accomplish the soul's mission.

Our souls exist on the soul plane. This is a dimension of light and vibration that is closer to Oneness, Universal energy, God, the All-That-Is, than the earth plane. Our souls are infused with spirit. Spirit is the consciousness that permeates and gives life to our souls, just as our souls permeate and give life to us. Our souls provide that medium through which spirit reaches us. It is the link between spirit and our personality.

Our souls are much more than a combination of our mental, emotional and physical bodies. It is the intelligence that directs the building of our bodies. It contains our essence between lifetimes and holds the patterns that created us in this lifetime. It has qualities of mind and mental awareness; it is intelligent and creative. It can draw matter to itself to create forms in our physical world. It lives in higher spiritual dimensions and brings the light and energy of those dimensions to us.

Our souls are not separate from us. They are a part of us. When we make soul contact we begin to know our selves as souls. We must expand consciousness in order to experience our soul's light, wisdom and love.

Our souls are made of light and are the embodiment of love. They are masters on their own plane, the soul plane. To grow and fulfill their higher purpose, our souls need to become masters of the physical plane in which we live. Part of their purpose is to learn how to send their light into our personalities, mind and emotions in order to establish higher light and rhythm. Our personality is an expression of our soul as it exists on the earth plane in the world of form and matter. Our level of spiritual evolution is determined by the mastery that our soul has gained on the earth plane. Our soul's mastery on the earth plane comes from our ability to become one with it and to know and carry out its goals and purpose.

To reach enlightenment and authentic power, we cannot sit around and wait for our souls to contact us and do all the work for us. Our souls are in a state of deep meditation. Most of our soul's attention is turned upward toward the realms of Spirit, of pure God-light, until we are ready to call its attention to us. Although it is always transmitting waves of soul energy to us, its work with us changes when we develop an awareness of it. Then we can use its stimulating, purifying, and transformative energies to grow spiritually.

We are the ones who need to draw our soul's attention to us. We do this through expanding our consciousness, seeking to be our higher selves, growing spiritually, and awakening our light bodies. We draw our souls to us through our will and our intention to make our inner life real. When we consciously connect with our souls and continually draw it into our lives, our souls begin to put more attention and energy into us. When this happens our spiritual growth accelerates rapidly. We work from the earth plane upwards, and our souls work from the soul plane downwards. As we blend with our soul we can absorb its spiritual knowledge. This will improve our daily life. Our soul knows the divine plan for humanity and for all life; it knows the part we are to play in that plan.

As the soul sends its light downward, it experiences itself through our earth consciousness. It can better express itself through us as our personality becomes more conscious and responsive to the soul. The soul can fulfill its higher purpose of mastering and bringing its light into the world of form and matter that we live in. As we blend with our soul and radiate its energy in our daily life, we serve humanity in a more valuable way. We become distributors of soul energy. Through soul contact, we will radiate love, light, beauty, and joy to others.

Preparing for the Journey to Our Soul

To fuse with our soul we must take a journey to the soul plane. This journey takes place on the mental level. We have to prepare ourselves for this journey as we would any other. If we were going to a new country, we would want to make sure we have the appropriate attire and equipment; change our money to the right currency of that country; learn the language or make provision for not speaking the language, create the time to be there, and prepare physically, mentally, and emotionally for the joys and challenges that lay ahead.

In the soul plane we will meet and blend with our soul. We will become familiar with a world made of light, learn a language that is composed of symbols and images and is transmitted telepathically, and use a currency of love. We will need to take a break from our daily routines and find a special time and a special place to visit and be in the soul plane. This special journey is usually referred to as, meditation, quiet time and prayer. Like most journeys we take, we may not realize the full value while we are there and we may not even consciously recognize the true value. However, as we make frequent visits to the soul plane we will see our life transform and we will get in touch with our authentic power and our life's purpose. Connecting with our souls will expand our consciousness, changing the way we think, feel, live and relate to others and ourselves.

Gaining the Co-operation of our Inner Child

In order to gain access to the soul we must resolve any opposition with any part of our personality. Our personality is composed of various parts. For example, there may be a rebellious self, a fearful self, an obedient self, a confident self, an insecure self, an adult self, a childlike self and so on. This is our inner child and it makes up our personality. This inner child acts like a sub- personality that appears sometimes for specific reasons.

As we have seen in chapter 12 our inner child was developed in our childhood, when we decided what was best for us based upon who we were as children, the environment we found ourselves in and the goals we had at that time. These goals may be very out of date and we must update them to have them cooperate with us in our journey to authentic power. Any time we find ourselves resisting soul contact or any of our goals, we need to take time to discover any inner child whose fears, doubts, and concerns need to be heard and evolved, in order to gain its cooperation. The inner child can change from resisting what we want to actively assisting us in getting it.

In order to contact and evolve your inner child, you need to get into a meditative mood. Start by relaxing your body, breath deeply and rhythmically, calm your emotions and quiet your mind. Become your higher self – wise, all knowing, compassionate, calm, and centered. The higher self is the self that is cooperating with the soul to bring our soul's wisdom to all parts of our personality. We need to use our imagination to picture our selves acting, thinking, and feeling as if we are our higher selves.

When we are settled and ready we must invite the part of us that is resisting and is not ready to meet our soul to come to us. We must pay attention to what this inner child looks, feels and acts like. We must notice everything we can about it. We must allow it to come to us and we must listen to it. What is its concern? Discover all that we can about it. We must feel the powerful unconditional love our higher self has for our inner child. We must then embrace the inner child with our love and send it light and energy. We must watch it grow more beautiful the more energy we give it. We must then show this part of ourselves the expanded view of our life. Let it see how much more there is to our life than this inner child has seen up to now.

Ask our inner child what good things it is trying to do for us. All our inner children are trying to do something good for us even if it appears that they are resisting us. Thank it for the good it is trying to do for you. Share with your inner child your present goals and plans, such as blending with your soul and expanding your ability to love. Ask this inner child if it has any fears of your plans and goals. Tell it that it will still have an important role to play in your life and ask it to assist you in creating your new plans and goals. Notice how this inner child changes as it grows and softens, and gains a new understanding of who you are and who you want to be. Continue to send it energy and light until it agrees to work with you in attaining your present goals, dreams and plans.

Journey to the Soul Plane

There are many planes of reality, from the physical earth plane we live in to the higher dimensions where everything is made of light. In this earth plane, life force, time, matter, and energy come together in certain ways to form the reality we know. In the soul plane, time is simultaneous, light has a different quality, and matter as we know it, does not exist.

We can sense the soul plane and our soul by expanding our consciousness. There are many ways to expand our consciousness to reach the soul plane. They include entering into a meditative state, using sound and chanting, and working with a spiritual guide. All involve achieving states where the body is relaxed, our emotions are calm, and the mind is clear.

Focusing on the solar light is a powerful and effective way to expand our consciousness to reach the soul plane. The solar light is the light from the soul of the physical sun. It sustains all life on the soul plane – in a similar way that our physical sun sustains all life on the physical plane. The light is a vast, magnificent being. Its energy reaches into many higher dimensions and shines through to the earth plane. It is the sum total of all consciousness on the soul plane and all planes below it, including the earth plane. The solar light is a light of beauty, perfection, and love. We can use our inner eye and imagination to picture the solar light. We can feel and think of it and it will expand our consciousness and guide us to the soul.

We must then bring this soul light into our awareness. Going to the solar plane is a journey of expansion rather than a journey of movement. We must call this solar light to ourselves and surround ourselves with it. Continue to relax and rise to the soul plane by playing with your breathing and making your body comfortable. Keep absorbing solar light, drawing it into your cellular structure.

Meeting Our Soul

In the soul plan we can travel anywhere by making a picture of where we want to be. We can call our soul to us by sounding an inner note. There is a part of us that knows exactly how to do this. We have actually sounded this note many times before, when we called out for greater strength, wisdom, love, or assistance. Our soul came to us in those moments and blended its light with ours to increase our inner knowingness, strength, and courage. It is these times when we wonder how we did what we did. We are now requesting that our soul become a permanent part of our consciousness and establish more of its presence in our daily life.

Find the note you can sound from deep within you that calls your soul. This note tells your soul that you are ready. Your soul will know your intention to meet it. It will hear your call and come. When your soul hears your call it will respond to you. It may become mentally visible, or you may feel its presence. Acknowledge the power of this moment. Feel the rush of energy and the sense of contact as your soul turns its attention to you. Discover how beautiful, magnificent, and powerful your soul is. Feel its vastness and its love. This is part of you. Your soul is an exquisite, wonderful, and divine being. It has so much love for you. Send your love to it, and open the rest of yourself to receive its love for you.

Greet your soul as a living presence of great love, wisdom, and intelligence. Move your awareness into your soul and it will transform your consciousness.

When our awareness is fully inside of our soul, we will experience a profound stillness. We need to allow the stillness of the luminous light to flow through us. This light of spirit has the power to transform us at every level. As we observe this luminous light in the center of our soul, it brings clarity of mind. It connects us to the very essence of our being. Every time we think of it, feel it, or sense it, we are transforming our consciousness.

Living as our Soul

Once we have called our soul to us and we are fully aware of our soul, our next step is to blend the personality with the soul. As the blending process takes place we will become radiant with soul light. We will feel and sense our soul's light, lighting up our highest path and creating light all about us. We will receive this beautiful light into our heart and mind. The soul will bring new thoughts, ideas, and creative inspiration to us.

When we blend with our soul, we will access the unlimited power, love, and light of our soul. While our most powerful experience of the soul may come in a state of meditation, once we have done that, we can learn to call upon it during ordinary moments, sense its presence, and make it part of our daily life. With practice we can call the soul to us, blend with it and experience its presence just by thinking about it. Blending with our soul throughout the day will greatly enhance our ability to live as our soul. Working with our soul is an important step to take on our journey of authentic power and enlightenment. We need to blend with our soul as often as possible to learn how its presence can change our lives for the better. Make soul contact often so that the soul's presence, power, light, love, will, and other qualities can become more a part of our daily lives.

Our soul knows much more than our personalities. For example it knows other souls. We can be observant around other people and see what our soul is telling us about them. We can feel the sensations that the soul is transmitting.

To live as your soul is to start imagining that you are your soul. Ask yourself, "What would I, as my soul, do in this area of my life? What actions would I take that would reflect my soul's purpose, vision and goals?" Mentally ask your soul, "How can I open to receive more of your energy and love? "How can I serve you in accomplishing your goals? How might I work with you more effectively? Although we may not receive direct answers, by simply asking these questions we open our minds for new insights and understandings.

Soul Mates

Soul mates are loved ones we have in our lives, who are responsive to our love, and who can match our new level of love. It is people who we are deeply connected with and who share a common path, purpose and who we can build a soul relationship with.

Most of us have more than one soul mate. We may have already been in several soul mate relationships with friends and loved ones. A soul mate can come in the form of a life partner, treasured friend, child, parent, or lover. A soul mate can be someone with whom we share a spiritual path, a joint work in the world, or a commitment to be parents to certain souls. It can be someone whose growth we are sponsoring, such as a child.

A soul mate can be someone who came to learn similar lesson as ours. Or, it can be someone who came to learn from us. Or, it can be someone who came to teach us something along our path. A soul mate can be someone who is connected to us from a past lifetime with whom we are continuing to develop a past life relationship.

Most of us choose to be in soul mate relationships with other souls that are in a similar stage of development as our soul. Thus the soul mate will be growing at the same rate and learning the same things. We will be challenged to learn the soul quality of self-love. The degree to which we love ourselves will determine our ability to love the other person. The other person will be like a mirror reflecting back to us our own personality traits and qualities. We will need to be vulnerable and let the other into our heart. We will grow by letting go of blame and self-pity, and by recognizing that we can only receive from the other what we can give ourselves.

Soul Mate as Life Partner

If we want to attract a soul mate as a life partner, there are many beliefs and illusions that we have to let go of. The first is that our soul mate is someone we are going to be with us for the rest of our lives. We can have a soul mate relationship that lasts a few weeks, months or years. Linear time has nothing to do with the quality of our connection and its importance in our lives. We may be in a soul mate relationship that lasts for the rest of our live on this plane. Or, we may have learned all we came together to learn in a matter of months. We should not measure the importance of a relationship based on the length of time we are together.

Second, we need to let go of the illusion that there is only one soul mate that is our true life partner. Some of us may have already had a soul mate connection with a life partner, sharing a caring, loving, bond that created much growth for us. Just because the outer bond has ended does not mean that it was not a soul mate relationship for us. There are many possible soul mate relationships that could be right for us, if the time is right for us to have a soul mate in our life. Who we attract at a given time will depend on the path we choose for ourselves and whether or not the other person is ready for a soul mate relationship.

Third, we will need to let go of the illusion that there is a perfect person waiting for us, who will fulfill our every expectation and give our personality everything it desires once we are together. Do not expect your ideal soul mate to be someone who is always loving and easy to get along with, who agrees with everything you say or do, and who brings you a life of ease and comfort. We may experience our soul mate like that at times and at other times our soul mate may challenge us to love as our soul loves.

You next need to make sure that you have no belief that will inhibit your soul mate from coming to you. Beliefs are conclusions you have made about the nature of reality. Beliefs can cancel the magnetic work of the heart, or they can reinforce your magnetism and assist you in drawing your soul mate to you. Release any negative thoughts you may have such as, "There is no one available who is as evolved as I am, who is interested in the same things as I am." Release any idea that you are unlovable or that there is no one available for you.

Work with all your limiting beliefs to change them. Tell yourself that there are souls who are evolved as you are and that it can be easy to meet a soul mate. Catch any negative thought you have and change it to a positive one.

Meeting our Soul Mate on the Soul plane

When we feel ready to meet our mate — we must enter the soul plane and call our soul to us and blend with it. We must think of the relationship that we want or we can ask our soul to use its wisdom in drawing to us the soul mate whom is best for us to meet and grow with at this time. Our soul knows exactly what to do to call this soul to us. Observe and feel as one of the souls in the sea of light comes to you. Observe and feel the connection, recognition and beauty of the moment. You have connection with the soul of your soul mate.

Radiate love to this person's soul. Receive love as this person's soul radiates love to you. Sense the beautiful patterns of light you can form together. Mentally ask this person's soul if this person is ready to meet with you face-to-face. Does this person need time to prepare for you or, is this person ready to meet with you soon? The answer may come as a feeling or inner knowing.

When you are ready to welcome your soul mate into your life, you can do so through you magnetic heart center. Let your soul fill your heart center with so much love that your heart center becomes like a magnet, radiating a powerful, magnetic love. Then soul link with your soul mate. Allow streams of living love to flow out of your heart center to your soul mate magnetizing this person to you, calling him or her into your life. If the person you have chosen is right for you and you are both ready – it will just be a matter of time before this person is brought into you life.

CHAPTER 19

THE NATURE OF GOD

Our conception and understanding of God affects our lives in every way — we need to develop an empowering conception of God.

We as a species, have been asking questions about the existence of God such as, "Is there a God?" "What is the nature of God?" "Is there a divine intelligence?" "Is there more than one God?" "Is there a purpose to life?", for as long as we have been able to ask questions. The time has now come for us to expand into a frame of reference that allows us to answer these questions.

Understanding the nature of God is fundamental to actualizing our authentic power and achieving our full human potential. One of our biggest problems is the fact that we have erroneous conceptions of God. We have paradigms of God that do not support our growth and our personal development. Deprogramming some of these erroneous conceptions of God is one of the most important steps towards personal growth and closer intimacy with God. The fact that the existence of God is so often questioned and that divine presence is so rarely experienced within the human soul is the result of the distorted images of God most of us entertain.

Truth

In any conversation about God, one of the first things that we must get a hold of is an understanding of the concept of "truth". Most of us believe in something as the "truth", be it our religion, our culture or some scientific or philosophical teaching. We hold this to be the truth and oppose anything that contradicts or is different from our beliefs. This notion is particularly problematic because "truth" just is and cannot be reduced to language. Once we start to describe it or to put it in our human language – it is no longer the truth, but a description of the truth. Richard Rorty in his book, Contingency, Irony, and Solidarity, captured this notion beautifully; He wrote:

> "We need to make a distinction between the claim that the world is out there and the claim that truth is out there. To say that the world is out there, that it is not our creation, is to say, with common sense, that most things in space and time are the effects of causes which do not include human mental states. To say that truth is not out there is simply to say that where there are no sentences there is no truth, that sentences are elements of human languages, and that human languages are human creations.
>
> Truth cannot be out there — cannot exist independently of the human mind — because sentences cannot so exist, or be out there. The world is out there, but descriptions of the world are not. Only descriptions of the world can be true or false. The world on its own — unaided by the describing activities of human beings — cannot.
>
> The suggestion that truth, as well as the world, is out there is a legacy of an age in which the world was seen as the creation of a being who had a language of his own. If we cease to

attempt to make sense of the idea of such a nonhuman language, we shall not be tempted to confuse the platitude that the world may cause us to be justified in believing a sentence true with the claim that the world split itself up, on its own initiative, into sentence-shape chunks called "facts." But if one clings to the notion of self-subsistent facts, it is easy to start capitalizing the word "Truth" and treating it as something identical either with God or with the world as God's project. Then one will say, for example, that Truth is great, and will prevail."

THE FALSE CONCEPTION OF GOD

False conceptions of God start from when we are children. Children experience their first conflict with authority at a very early age. They also learn that God is the highest authority figure. Therefore it is not surprising that children project their subjective experience with authority unto their imagining about God. Hence a wrong conclusion is formed about God, which is unconsciously carried into adulthood.

Children experience all types of authority figures. The main authority figures are their parents. When they are prohibited from doing what they enjoy most, they experience authority as hostile. When parenting authority indulges a child, authority will then occur as benign. When there is predominance of one kind of authority in childhood the reaction to that will become the unconscious attitude towards God.

To the extent that the child experiences fear and frustration, to that extent will fear and frustration subconsciously be felt towards God. God is then believed to be a punishing, severe and often even an unfair and unjust God that one has to contend with. All of this will combine to make a monster out of God. In fact the God living in most of our subconscious minds is more of a Satan.

If this subconscious conception of God becomes conscious it oftentimes will find such a person moving away from God and wanting no part of this monster of a God. This is often the true reason of someone's atheism. The turning away is just as erroneous as the opposite extreme which consists of fearing a God who is severe, unjust, pious, self righteous and cruel. The person who subconsciously maintains this distorted God image rightly fears this deity and resorts to cajoling for favors. Here you have a good example of two opposite extremes both of which lack truth to an equal extent.

Now let us examine the other case where a child experiences benign authority to a greater degree than fear and frustration with a negative authority. Let us assume that overindulging parents fulfill the child's every need. They do not instill a sense of responsibility in the child, who gets get away with practically anything. The God image resulting in such a condition is, at first superficial sight, closer to the true concept of God — forgiving, good, loving and indulgent. This causes the personality to unconsciously think that he or she can get away with anything in the eyes of God, and therefore can cheat life, and avoid responsibility. But since life cannot be cheated, this wrong attitude will produce conflict and therefore fear will be generated by a chain reaction of wrong thinking, feeling and acting.

Many subdivisions and combinations of these two exist - of the benign authority of God or the fearful nature of God. In many instances children experience a mixture of both. Then the combinations of these two forms of authority will form their image of God. It is very important that we find out what our God image is. This image is basic and determines all other attitudes, images and pattern throughout our lives. We must not be deceived by our conscious convictions, rather we must examine and analyze our emotional reaction to authority, to our parents, to our fears and our expectations. Out of these we will gradually discover what we feel about God rather than what we think.

Deprogramming the God Image

Now the question of how to deprogram such an image arises. How do we deprogram any image, that is, any wrong conclusion? First, we have to become fully conscious of the wrong concept. The second step is to set our intellectual ideas straight. It is most important to understand that the proper formation of the intellectual concept should never be superimposed and still linger on the emotional false concept. This would only cause suppression. Realize that the hitherto suppressed wrong concept has to evolve clearly into consciousness to formulate the right concept. Then these two should be compared. We need constantly to check how much we still deviate emotionally from the right intellectual concept.

This is something that has to be done quietly, without inner haste or anger at ourselves that our emotions do not follow our thinking as quickly as we would like. We have to give our emotions time to grow. Constant observation and comparison of the wrong and the right concept best accomplish this. We must realize that our emotions need time to adjust. We must also observe our resistance to change and growth. We must be wise to the fact that the lower self of the human personality is very shrewd.

God is not unjust. We have to see the connection with our own law of cause and effect and this alone will set us free and show us that there is no injustice in the universe. It is not God, fate, or circumstances that cause us to suffer: it is our own ignorance, fear, pride and egotism that directly or indirectly cause us to suffer. If we find this hidden link then we can come to this truth. Emotions are very powerful creative forces, because our unconscious affects the unconscious of other people. This truth is most relevant in understanding how we cause the situations in our life, good or bad, favorable or unfavorable.

Once we experience this we can dissolve our God image. First we fear God because we believe that we live in a world of injustice and are afraid of being the prey of circumstances over which we have no control. Second we reject self responsibility and expect an over indulgent and pampering God to lead our lives for us, make decisions for us, and take self inflicted hardship from us. The realization of how we cause the effect of our lives will dissolve either God image whether it is good or bad. This is one of the main breaking points of to self responsibility and accountability.

THE TRUE CONCEPT OF GOD

God is. God's laws are made once and for all and work automatically. Think of God as universal energy that permeates every aspect of existence. We may think of God as a kind of electric current, endowed with supreme intelligence. This electric current is there in us, around us and outside of us. It is up to us how we use it. We can use electricity for constructive purposes, even for healing or we can use it to kill. That does not make the electric current good or bad. We make it good or bad. The power current is an important aspect of God and is one that touches us most.

This concept of God raises the question of whether God is personal or impersonal, a directing intelligence or law and spirit and principle. Since we human beings experience life in a dualistic sense, we tend to believe that one or the other must be true. Yet both are true: God is both personal and impersonal. But God's personal aspect does not mean a personality. God is not a person residing in a certain place. However, it is possible to have a personal God experience within the self, for the only place that God can be looked for and found is within, not in any other place.

God's existence can be deduced outside of the self, from the beauty of creation, from the manifestation of nature, from the wisdom collected by philosophers and scientists. But such observation becomes an experience of God only when God's presence is first felt within. The inner experience of God is the greatest of all experiences because it contains all the desirable experiences. An experience of God within is what we would call a cosmic feeling.

The cosmic feeling is not a theoretical understanding or a feeling about the cosmo or a feeling about the God image. The cosmic feeling is a true physical, mental, emotional and spiritual experience, which encompasses the entire person. This experience cannot adequately be described within the limitations of language. The cosmic experience is unity. It does not separate between the physical, the emotional, the mental and the spiritual. It doesn't split off feeling from thinking. It is feeling and thinking in one. This is very hard to imagine when we have never had such an experience. But some of us have occasionally had a glimpse of it. The oneness is total, it is an experience of bliss. It is the comprehension of life and its mysteries of all-encompassing love and knowledge that all is well and there is nothing to fear.

In this state of cosmic feeling we experience the immediacy of the presence of God within us. The immediacy of this incredible powerful presence is at first shocking. The good feeling is shocking; it is literally an electric shock going through our entire system. Therefore the ego personality has to grow sufficiently strong and healthy so that it can acclimatize itself to the higher vibrations of the inner presence of God. This manifestation is then experienced as our eternal reality and state of our true identity.

Once we experience this deep cosmic feeling, we know in our deepest self that this is something that we already know.

We have only temporarily cut ourselves off from it, and that this is our true identity.

DIVINE LAW

God's love is not only personal as manifested within the human soul, but it is also universal and omnipresent as manifested in divine law. God's love leads ultimately into light and bliss, no matter how much we deviate from divine law. The more you deviate from divine law the more you get close to them by working in the misery and destruction that the deviation leads you into. The misery will cause you to turn around and approach God's law in one way or another. Some sooner, some later but all of us will eventually come to the point when we will understand that we cannot continue to deviate from divine law. Every one of us will come to the consciousness that we are cause and effect in our lives. We create our own misery or our own bliss. This is the love in God's law. God lets us deviate from the law if we wish. We are made in God's likeness. This means that we are completely free to choose. We are not forced to live in love and light, though we can if we wish. All this expresses the love of God.

When we have difficulty understanding the justice of the universe and the self-responsibility in our lives, do not think of God as he or she, rather think of God as the great creative power at our disposal. It is not God who is unjust, the injustice is caused by the wrong use of the great power at our disposal. If we start from that premise and meditate on it, and if from now on we seek to find where and how we have been abusing the power current in ourselves, God will answer us. When we discover the cause and effect in our lives, this discovery will have a tremendous effect on our lives. The greater the resistance to it at first the greater the victory. We have no idea how free it will make us, how safe and secure. We will understand the marvel of the creation of these laws, that let us, with the power current of life, do as we please in creating our own life. This will give us confidence and deep absolute knowledge that we have nothing to fear.

When speaking of God it is very important to understand that all divine aspects are duplicated in the human psyche, whose life and whose being rest upon the same conditions, principles and laws as those pertaining to cosmic intelligence. They are both the same in essence, differentiated only by degree. Actualizing our full potential means activating the maximum potential of God in us.

GOD IS YOU AND CREATES THROUGH YOU

God acts deliberately and spontaneously, directing intelligence through us. God does not act for us but through us. It is very important that we understand this subtle but decisive difference. When we have an erroneous approach to God in this respect, we expect God to act for us and we experience the inevitable disappointment. Then we conclude that there is no creator. If we could contact an outer deity – we could logically expect it to act for us. But waiting for a response outside of ourselves is focusing in the wrong direction.

When we contact God within the self, response must come and that is guaranteed. When we discover ourselves and consequently the role we play in creating our fate, we will truly come into our own. We will no longer be driven but will be masters of our destiny, no longer bound by forces we do not understand. We can deliberately use these powers in the most constructive way to express more of the best in us, expand to even greater potential, add more to life and therefore derive more from life.

We must discover the power and the freedom to master our lives by ourselves. If life forces us into our truth, virtually in order to save us from suffering, we wouldn't be free. The very meaning of freedom is that no force or constraint can be used, not even for good or desirable results. Such discovery must lead to the realization that we are masters over the universe to the exact degree that we master ourselves. This depends on a thorough knowledge of ourselves and the depth and width of the concept that our minds are capable of embracing.

Since we are created in the image of God, we too must create. We constantly do so. Whether or not we believe it we create our fates, our experiences, our lives, every thought, every reaction, and every emotion, every response, every intent, every action, every opinion, every motivation are creative forces. Ideas and intent expressed by conscious beings are the greatest force in the universe. This means that the power of spirit is superior to all other energies. If this power is used and understood according to its inherent law, it supersedes all other manifestations of power. No physical power can be as strong as the power of the spirit. With spirit and intelligence we are inherently capable of directing all of God's laws. It is through this capacity that God is truly experienced.

When we deliberately contact and request our higher selves which contain all divine aspects for guidance and inspiration and when we experience the result of the inner heart, we will know that God is present within us. We have to find out what distorted images we have of God and then be determined not to let them stand in the way of a total blissful and cosmic feeling. We have to make ourselves open to the true power of God. We have to take the words that the most high has given to us into our soul and into our life, let them fill our heart, and let them be instruments to liberate us from illusions.

The relationship between God and man was captured in a poem written by Robert Collier.

"To man has been given the job of

emulating his maker — of becoming a creator, finding new and broader and better ways through which to express the creative force in him. His is the work of creating beauty or bringing more comfort, of joy and happiness into the world.

You are a son of God, a creator. Therefore creation is expected of you. You are to spread seeds not merely of human kind but of intellect as well. You are to leave the world a better place than you found it, with more of joy in it, more of beauty, of comfort, of understanding, of light."

PART VI

OUR HUMAN POTENTIALS

Love
Power
Purpose
Prosperity

CHAPTER 20

Love

*Love is the only path towards spiritual
consciousness. This truth is not negotiable,
no matter what spiritual tradition we choose
as a means to know the Divine. Love is
Divine Power.*

I have been studying excellence, holistic healing, authentic power and transformation in human beings for a while, and have been asking myself "what is the fundamental principle that leads to excellence, and holistic healing?". What makes some people, especially children, do well and others not do so well? I was pleasantly surprised to discover that love is the first and most important step to holistic healing, transformation, success and authentic power. Furthermore, it is central to every spiritual teaching that I have encountered. The principle is love. In fact, Jesus' message and many messages from spiritual prophets can simply be summed up by the word "love". Most of us seem to believe that all we have to do is love God, and forget our neighbors, children and most of all, ourselves. Ironically, we are unaware that there is no love to give to anyone, including God, unless we first love ourselves. We cannot give away that which we do not have.

Children are able to sense this, as they cannot be fooled. You will find that in a family, it does not matter how much of this "false" love children receive, they can still turn out to be self-destructive. In fact, children have the most to gain by receiving love and the most to lose by the lack of it. It has recently been suggested that the reason some children perform better than others, has less to do the with the child's innate ability, or with his/her parents' financial position, and more to do with the amount of love that child receives. This is a very interesting proposition, because before we can love our children or anyone else, we must first love ourselves.

How do we actually start loving ourselves? Many of us want easy answers, but unfortunately, I don't believe there are any. I believe that there is a process, which involves deconstructing and removing some of the walls and fortresses we have built around our hearts and souls. Once we have shattered these fortresses and façades, our authenticity shows up and the entire world is different, not because the world has changed, but because we have.

Love heals physical illnesses

Much of what I am saying has now been confirmed by various scientific and sociological studies. Many new age healing institutions are now reporting that illnesses that were once considered incurable can now be healed once the patient changes his or her lifestyle and begins receiving as well as giving love into their lives. Fundamentally, we can cure or prevent any illness with love — because the real key to good health is love.

For example, researchers at Harvard Medical School have found that when we care for someone – or we are cared for – there is a sharp increase of a chemical in our blood, which helps to fight off illnesses. Further, medical specialists around the world now agree that the prescription for a healthier life is the affection of other people. The Director of the World Health Organization, Dr. Marsden Wagner, has stated that "Modern medicine has forgotten about the power of love."

In Israel, a researcher spent five years studying 10,000 men to see which of them developed angina, a painful heart ailment. Those who developed the disease all had one thing in common — their wives didn't show affection.

In California, doctors kept tabs on the population of a country, to try to learn what prevents people from getting sick. They found that the answer is not jogging, aerobic dancing or high protein diets, the secret, the doctors said, "is in having loving partners and close friends."

British heart specialists now believe that a lack of love is a bigger risk factor in cardiac disease than being too fat or chain smoking cigarettes. And as a cancer doctor who runs a clinic in Britain said: "Our outlook on life controls the way our body defenses work. And there is no doubt that they work best when we are happy and loved." He also said, "Happy family relationships are good for health, too."

A lot of mental and physical illnesses are linked to tensions within the family unit. When a family is racked with problems with children, financial shortcomings, and a multitude of other stress causing situations which exist mainly because the members don't know how to care for each other or communicate, mental and physical health seems to suffer. By learning how to give and receive love in our family unit we will be able to save lives and live much more happily.

In one Harvard experiment, all the patients in a hospital who were to have identical operations were visited by one of the doctors the night before their surgery. With some patients, the doctor asked routine questions while standing. With others, he/she sat on their beds or held their hands while standing. The study concluded that the patients who received the personal touch felt far less pain after the operation. They were also ready for discharge from the hospital three days earlier than those who received no personal attention.

All in all, a preponderance of evidence clearly suggests that love and the state of mind that is brought about by love can cure almost any ailment. We are by nature compassionate beings who thrive in an atmosphere of tranquillity and harmony. These energies are essential to physical health as well as to emotional development and acts of the heart. When the heart is not filled with the vital energies of love and harmony, no amount of money and power can keep it tranquil. An empty heart creates an empty life, often resulting in illness and dis-ease. Dis-ease is often times a concrete expression of disharmony that hopefully will get the mind's attention. We must rectify violations of the heart for true healing to occur.

Self-love

Through human relationships we grow and awaken. Our true loving nature emerges and expresses itself through our interaction with others in our family, social circle and professional life. No one is in our life by accident — each relationship comes with the same lesson: to teach love, for we are love.

We have happiness, joy, bliss and peace to the degree to which we love ourselves and extend love to others. We have high levels of health and energy to the extent to which we experience self-love, self-acceptance and have loving relationships with others. Love is also essential to our level of financial achievement in life. Most successful people do what they love to do. To the degree that we love ourselves and love what we are doing, we will set challenging and worthwhile goals to achieve. Self-love and self-acceptance make it easier to gain self-knowledge and self-understanding. Lasting self-fulfillment, self-expression and self-actualization in life is achieved only to the degree to which one loves and accepts oneself and others unconditionally.

We must first love ourselves unconditionally and our first marriage must be a symbolic one: a commitment to attend consciously to our own emotional needs, in order to love and accept others unconditionally. Learning to love ourselves unconditionally is a challenge to all of us. Most of us are inculcated in a paradigm of low self-love. We have to work toward it. When we neglect ourselves emotionally, we not only become emotionally toxic, we bring that toxin into all our relationships, particularly into our actual marriages.

Hugging

One of the most effective ways to include love in our lives on a daily basis is to practice hugging each other. When we hug another, emotional energy flows between our bodies. This energy is essential for sustaining life, love and authentic power.

Both our physical and emotional bodies need affection through hugging. If we do not hug, our physical and emotional bodies will be deprived and we will not be able to function at our maximum capacity. We need four hugs per day for our survival, eight hugs per day for a functional life and sixteen hugs per day for an extraordinary life. We need to practice hugging as part of our daily empowerment tool. It is an essential way to heal ourselves.

Children benefit most from hugging. If you want to raise functional children, you must make sure that you give them a healthy dose of hugging. A child who is not hugged enough will never be able to fully display love.

We should make a conscious effort to hug more each day. We should never let a day pass without hugging our children and loved ones. However, hugging should not remain only in the family, but we should extend it to as many people as we come in contact with daily. Hugging is a fundamental element of bringing more love, happiness and pleasure into our lives.

Love vs. Fear

Love is the opposite of fear. When we are not in a loving state, we are in a fearful state. There is no fear in love. Love casts out fear. Fear will rob us of love, happiness, and joy. The only way we can fulfill our full human potential is to diminish the role that fear plays in our lives and in our decisions. Our aim and our ideal must be to reach the point where we are not afraid of anything. When we eliminate fear, we become completely self-confident and our entire world opens up before us. Love will dissolve fear and remove it from our lives.

The greatest obstacles to the expression and experience of love are negative emotions, especially those of fear, resentment, anger, hate and guilt. Almost everyone is harboring negative emotions towards someone that has caused them hurt in the past. Many people carry around anger, guilt and resentment towards their parents for a lifetime. This not only prevents them from loving their parents, but also prevents them from loving themselves and others as well. People carry around resentment and anger years after failed relationships or business dealings. If a person clings to these negative emotions by dwelling upon them, he or she keeps them alive, years after the incident has passed.

LOVE AND SELF-ESTEEM

Self-esteem and self-respect are the fundamental qualities of a healthy personality. Everything we do to raise our self-esteem contributes to making us happier and more successful. Learning to love ourselves is the most effective method of building our self-esteem. We have to resolve to love and accept ourselves, no matter what we have done in our life to this point. We have to start loving ourselves, where we are, right now. We can like and respect ourselves exactly as we are rather than as we would like to be. The foundation of self-esteem is self-acceptance. The more we love ourselves, the more we will love other people. The more love we have for ourselves is the more love that we can give to others. We cannot give away that which we do not have.

The fastest way to boost our self-esteem and self-love is

to simply repeat fifty times a day — "I love myself" "I love myself" - until we implant this message deep into our subconscious mind. Eventually, our subconscious mind will fully accept this instruction as our operative motif. Then we will notice the difference — our body language, our attitude, our self-expression, our tone of voice will all change for the better and become more authentic. We will feel more positive, optimistic and enthusiastic about ourselves and everything we do.

We can use positive affirmations. We can visualize ourselves as the very best person that we can possibly be. We can fill our mind and heart with positive messages of hope and aspiration. We can associate with positive, happy, goal-oriented people. These actions will significantly boost our self-esteem and help us to realize our full human potential.

Another way we can build self-esteem is to take good care of ourselves physically. When we eat healthy, nutritious foods and get adequate sleep and regular exercise, we feel better about ourselves. The better we take care of ourselves, the more self-respect and self-love we have. This feeling will spread into our relationships with others and we will automatically treat others well.

Sowing and Reaping Love

We cannot have more love for ourselves, than we express to others. Love only grows as it is expressed to others. The only way you can have more love for yourself is by giving it to others. The more you give away, the more you have. By the same token, the more you withhold love, the less you have for yourself. The more you give love away — the more it comes right back to you.

The happiest men and women in the world are those that continually look for ways to give and show love, kindness, and affection towards life. As a result of being loved and respected by others — they are the happiest, healthiest and most blessed of all human beings.

Love is an active verb. Love is something to do. The only true measure of our belief is our action. It is not so much what we say, or what we wish, feel or hope that counts, but what we actually do. It is action, not words, that count the most. There are many specific things we can do that combine to build within us the feelings of high self-esteem and self-regard that make everything else possible. But the fundamental principle is that the more we give love the more we get love. If you want more love, just give more love.

LOVE AND FORGIVENESS

The main doorway that opens a life of love, joy, happiness and peace of mind is forgiveness. Our ability to freely forgive other people, and to let the hurt go, is the true mark of integrity, courage, character and a fully developed personality. Forgiving others is a selfish act. We do it so that we can be free. We forgive so that we can experience the joy and the happiness for which we were created.

We can clear our hearts and minds of the negativity we have built up over time with one decisive action: issue a blanket pardon to everyone for everything that they have ever done to hurt us is any way whatsoever. We do not even have to tell them personally – it is more a matter of clearing ourselves of the negativity.

As appealing as forgiveness is in theory, it is an unattractive personal action for most people, mainly because the true nature of forgiveness is predominantly misunderstood. Forgiveness is not the same as telling the person who harmed you, "It's okay," which is more or less the way most people view it. Rather, forgiveness is a complex act of consciousness, one that liberates the psyche and soul from the need for personal vengeance and the perception of oneself as a victim.

More than releasing us from the blame of those persons

who caused our wounds, forgiveness means releasing the control, that the perception of victimhood has over our psyches. The liberation that forgiveness generates comes in the transition to a higher state of consciousness. The consequence of a genuine act of forgiveness borders on the miraculous.

Forgiveness is an essential spiritual act that must occur in order to open ourselves fully to the healing power of love. Self-love means caring for ourselves so much that we forgive people in our past so that the wounds can heal and no longer damage us. Our wounds do not hurt the people who hurt us – they hurt only us. Releasing our attachment to these wounds enables us to move from childish relationships into mature adult relationships in which we act out of love and compassion.

I love the following poem by Robert Muller about forgiveness. I believe that it captures the essence of forgiveness.

"Decide to forgive
For resentment is negative
Resentment is poisonous
Resentment diminishes and devours the self.
Be the first to forgive,
To smile and to take the first step,
And you will see happiness bloom
On the face of your human brother or sister.
Be always the first
Do not wait for others to forgive
For by forgiving
You become the master of fate
The fashioner of life
The doer of miracles.
To forgive is the highest,
Most beautiful form of love.

In return you will receive
Untold peace and happiness."

Love is the foundation of authentic power. Our bodies, minds and spirits need love to survive and strive. We violate this energy when we act towards others and ourselves in unloving ways. When we harbor negative emotions toward ourselves, or when we intentionally create pain for others, we poison our own human physical, mental and spiritual systems. By far the strongest poison to our spiritual body is the inability to forgive others and ourselves. Resentments disable our emotional resources.

Love and trust are one and the same. You cannot have one without the other. Any belief otherwise is an illusion. Love and trust are the opposite of fear. When we do not love and trust we fear. And as we have seen, fear is the greatest immobilizer of human potential.

The Love Cycle
I trust, love, forgive and accept myself so much
That I can trust, love, forgive and accept you so much
That you can trust, love, forgive and accept
yourself so much
So that you can trust, love, forgive and accept me.

LOVE IS THE GREATEST
One of the most beautiful and pointed descriptions of love that I have seen comes from the Christian Bible in First Corinthians, Chapter Thirteen. It is as follows:

Though I speak with tongues of men and of
angels and have not love, I am become as
sounding brass, or a tinkling cymbal. And though

Love I have the gift of prophecy, and understand all mysteries, and all knowledge; and though I have all faith, so that I could remove mountains, and have not love, I am nothing.

And though I bestow all my goods to the poor, and though I give my body to be burned, and have not love, it profiteth me nothing.

Love suffereth long, and is kind; love envieth not; love vaunteth not itself, is not puffed up, Love does not behave itself unseemly, love seeketh not her own, love is not easily provoked, and love thinketh no evil; Love rejoiceth not in iniquity, but rejoiceth in the truth; Love beareth all things, beliveth all things, hopeth all things, endureth all things.

Love never faileth; but whether there be prophecies, they shall fail; whether there be tongues, they shall cease; whether there be knowledge, it shall vanish away. For we know in part, and we prophesy in part. But when that which is perfect is come, then that which is in part shall be done away.

When I was a child, I spake as a child, I understood as a child, I thought as a child: but when I became a man, I put away childish things. For now we see through a glass, darkly; but then face to face: now I know in part; but then shall I know even as also I am known.

And now abideth faith, hope, charity, these three, but the greatest of these is love."

When we become totally loving human beings we will understand all, forgive all, and experience true joy in every part of our lives.

Loving as our Souls

The greatest way we can experience love is to connect with our souls and to love as our souls. We must first open ourselves to receive love from our souls. When we connect with our souls and accept its love, we are connecting with an infinite supply of love energy. As we accept our soul's love we can say to ourselves, "I deserve love. I now allow unlimited love and light into my life." As we accept love from our souls we develop the ability to receive. Our growing ability to receive love can allow us to embrace all the gifts the universe and our souls have to offer us. We must also notice and appreciate all the good things we already have. Gratitude draws even more good things to us from our souls and the universe.

We must open to receive our soul's love as often as we can. Our souls know that we are magnificent and wonderful beings. It loves our humanness and our divinity. It is incapable of judging us, of being mad at, disappointed in, or being angry with us. It celebrates every time we love ourselves and each other – knowing that as we love and honor each other and ourselves, we grow closer to it. Our soul loves and accepts us unconditionally, without exceptions.

CHAPTER 21

POWER

Authentic power is internal power; it comes from the center of our being. It is an energy that is formed from the intentions of our souls. This power is a light from our highest self and it leads us to accomplish our life's purpose.

Power is a very emotional word. Many people have a very unhealthy relationship with power. Our responses to it are varied. For some of us, power has a negative connotation. Some of us lust after power. Others feel tainted by it, as if it was somehow venal or suspect. How much power do you have? How much power do you want? How much power do you think is right for you to obtain or develop? What does power really mean to you?

The power to control the physical world and those within it is power of the five senses – that is power that can be felt, smelled, tasted, heard or seen. This is exoteric or external power. This type of power can be bought, sold, inherited, won, or transferred. It can be gotten from someone or somewhere else other than from oneself.

This perception is that there is a scarcity of power. When one person gains, another person loses. This results in a tug-o-war for power, which brings with it violence, greed, envy and destruction. Many of our institutions – political, economic, social and even some religious ones — view power in this external way.

Money and material things are symbols of external power. The more money you have, the more you believe you? are able to control your environment and those in it. Anything that you derive a sense of security from – such as education, career, spouse, social status, fame or things that one owns, are symbols of external power. Anything that you fear to lose, a spouse, a home, a car, a job, an attractive body is a symbol of external power. What you fear is an increase in vulnerability, which results from viewing power as external.

I don't think of power in terms of conquering, dominating or exploiting people. I don't think of it as something to be imposed on others at all. I'm not suggesting that you should, either. That kind of power is fear based and seldom lasts. It is the ego's attempt to compensate for our deeply held fears, insecurities and sense of unworthiness.

We must realize that power is a constant in the world. We shape our perception and reality, or someone shapes them for us. We do what we want to do, or we react to someone else's plan for us. To me, personal power is the ability to accomplish our life's purpose and produce the results we desire most, while creating value for others.

Personal power is the ability to change our life, to shape our perceptions, to make things work for us and not against us. Real power is shared, not imposed. It's the ability to define human needs and to fulfill them — both our needs and the needs of the people we care about. It's the ability to direct our own personal kingdom — our own thought processes, our own behavior — so we produce the precise results we desire.

Soul Power

A deeper understanding of life leads to another kind of power, a power that loves life in every form that it appears, a power that does not judge what it encounters. When we align our bodies, emotions, thoughts and actions with the highest part of ourselves, we are filled with enthusiasm, purpose and meaning to our lives. This is authentic power. Life is exciting, rich, challenging and full; we have no memory or thought of bitterness or fear. This is the experience of genuine soul based power.

A good way to determine whether our power is ego based or soul based is to determine what we stand for. We are only as powerful as what we stand for. If we stand for more money, a bigger house, an attractive spouse, imposing our will on others, then our power is ego based. This is the ego seeking to satisfy itself. On the other hand if we stand for love, integrity, beauty, perfection, clarity, forgiveness, humbleness and wisdom, then we are standing for the power of the soul. This is the stand of an ego that has aligned itself with the power of the soul. This is genuine and authentic power.

Authentic power is esoteric or internal power; it comes from the center of our being. It is an energy that is formed from the intentions of the soul. This power is a light from our highest self and it leads us to accomplish our life's purpose. It helps to develop the ego towards the accomplishment of our task on earth.

Authentic power is simply the energy of the soul. Everything is energy. Therefore the soul is energy. Souls are in a constant exchange of energy. Whenever we are close to someone, we exchange energy with him or her. Whenever we think and feel something about someone we are exchanging energy with him or her. When we are expressing fear or any negative emotion, energy leaves us in an incorrect way and it exhausts our being – physically, emotionally, mentally and spiritually.

For example, if someone is experiencing fear about his or her job, he or she will experience discomfort or pain in the stomach area. This is caused from energy leaving the body from that energy center. Also if we experience fears or doubts about a relationship, we will experience pain or discomfort in the heart area – this is what we call heartache – and is caused by energy leaving the heart from the heart center. Heartache is the loss of power through your heart center – this can lead to what we call a heart attack.

Every illness – physical, mental or emotional – can be traced to the loss of energy to an external circumstance or object through one or several energy centers in the body. We lose power when we fight, quarrel, rage, become angry, resent, long for someone or something, grieve, envy, or hate. Beneath all of these negative emotions, is a fear. We lose power every time we fear – that is what a loss of power is.

As we have already learned, the idea is not to suppress our feelings. We do not stop losing power by anesthetizing ourselves to our feelings. The way to authentic power is through our heart – it is through what we feel. We must become conscious of what we feel – because that is the only way we can challenge our fears, resolve them and move into positive emotions and vibrations.

When we stop losing our power in a negative way, we will become a stable energy system – who is capable of conscious, focused acts and intentions. We will become captivating to those who are illumined and an inspiration to those who are on the path. The question is, how does energy leave our body? If it leaves our body as fear, or any negative emotion, it can only bring us pain and discomfort. On the other hand if it leaves our body as love and trust it returns with power, comfort and self-actualization.

Live in the Moment

An authentically empowered person lives in the moment. When we are caught up worrying about the past and the future, we are losing energy to circumstances and events that do not exist and have no power over us. The past is history and the future is mystery. The present moment is our only reality. An authentically empowered person learns how to live in the moment. If we want to have an extraordinary life, the place to start is to start having extraordinary moments. If we live each moment with love, integrity and gratitude we will experience authentic power.

Relax into the present moment. Do what you need to do now. Do not worry about the future. That does not mean you should not consider the consequences of our choices. Remember, what we have learned about responsible choice: it means to create strongly in the present moment. Do not lose power over the "what-ifs" of your life. Keep your power in the now, in the present moment and do not worry about the past or the future. Challenge your worry each time it comes up, by literally realizing that when it comes up, you are not engaged in your present energy dynamics, but rather you are allowing energy to leak to a future that does not exist.

LOVE AND POWER

Love, trust and forgiveness are the fundamental characteristics of authentic power. These principles are the energy of the soul.

Love is the energy of the soul. Love heals everything. There is nothing but love. Love is an active force. Love brings peace, harmony and unification. It brings trust, forgiveness, acceptance, happiness and bliss. A positive emotion is like light. A negative emotion is darkness – illusion — or the absence of light. Once there is light, there is no darkness. Once there is love and positive emotions, there is no fear and the negative emotions – because all negative emotions are illusions. There is only love.

An authentically powerful person learns to forgive. Only through forgiveness can we truly love. We cannot love someone we have not forgiven. We cannot truly love ourselves until we forgive ourselves. Most people think of forgiveness as a moral issue, but it is not – it is an energy dynamic. When we do not forgive, the experience that we do not forgive sticks with us. We hold others responsible and accountable for our own wants, feelings and experiences. We lose power. When we do not forgive, we whine and complain that others will not devote themselves to making us happy.

Forgiveness means that we let go of the negative emotions surrounding the issue and therefore stop losing our energy in a negative way. It means that we no longer carry the baggage of the experience. It means that we do not hold others responsible for our feelings and experiences. When we forgive, we hold ourselves accountable and responsible for what we feel and experience. We can then share what we feel and experience in a spirit of companionship and love. Forgiveness is blameless and non-judgmental. It releases all critical judgement of ourselves and others. We lighten up. We learn to laugh at our mistakes and past indiscretions – learning from the lessons they carry. We release all regrets and doubts. We cultivate a dancing, happy heart.

Trust is the most powerful principle on the journey to authentic power and actualizing our full human potential.

All that we have discussed is the prerequisite for movement into trust. What is trust? And which part of our being should we trust?

Before we came to this particular lifetime, each soul agreed to perform a certain task while here. The soul enters into an agreement to accomplish a goal. All our experiences, serve to remind us of that task and to prepare us to fulfill it. The unempowered ego cannot accomplish the task of the soul. No matter what the ego attains – it could become the richest man on earth – it will still languish in a state of emptiness, as long as it is not on the path of the soul. The sense of emptiness, of something missing, or of something wrong, cannot be filled by wants of the ego. This emptiness can only be filled when the personality begins to walk the path of the soul.

The universe is a friendly universe. We just need to trust it and it will move us in the right direction. Most of our problems come from lack of trust. We do not trust others, the universe, or ourselves. We insist on holding onto a doorknob that leads nowhere. When all we have to do is "let go and let God". Trust and create. The rest is up to the universe. Be able to say "thy will be done" and rest in the certainty that the universe will lead you in the right direction.

Trusting means that wherever we are – it is working towards our highest good. There is no when, where, how or if to it. It just is. Just trust that the universe is working for your every good. We need to say to the universe: "find me where I need to be"; "send me the people I need to meet". Let go of all and let spirit run your life. I am reminded of a song written and composed by Rickie Byars-Beckwith & Reverend Michael Beckwith, which goes like this:

> There was a time in my life
> I thought I had to do it all for myself
> I didn't know the Grace of God was sufficient
> I didn't know the LOVE of God was at hand
>
> Now I can say if you are discouraged
> Struggling just to make it through another day
> You've got to let it go, let it all go
> and this is what you have to say
>
> CHORUS:
>
> I release and I let go
> I let the SPIRIT run my life

> and my heart is open wide,
> Yes, I'm only here for God
>
> No more struggle, no more strife
> with my faith I see the light
> I am free in the SPIRIT
> Yes, I'm only here for GOD.

The journey to authentic power allows us to become conscious of all that we feel. We need to call forth all our negative feelings in order to heal them. The main door to our authentic power is through our heart. Feel not what your intellect tells you, but what your heart tells you. Do not serve the false Gods of your mind, serve the real God of your heart. Remember the kingdom of God is within you. You will not find God in your intellect. God is in your heart.

Our everyday activity is creating what is appropriate at our present level of evolution. When we apply consciousness to this process, we live consciously instead of unconsciously. Although what we experience in each moment is appropriate for the growth of our soul – the shape of our experiences are determined nonetheless by your choices. We can unconsciously live in the lower energy frequency of negativity, or we can consciously choose the higher frequency of positivity. Eventually all roads lead to home. If we choose hate, anger, resentment, or jealousy, we will still be led to love, but only through trauma, pain and a sense of loss. Our only choice is whether we grow consciously or unconsciously.

CHAPTER 22

PURPOSE

*Each of us has a compelling reason why
we incarnated at this time. This reason is
our purpose for this lifetime.*

Each of us has something special about us. Each of us has a unique vision, a meaning and purpose to our life, in which we can be the most successful, the most fulfilled, and the happiest. The discovery and fulfillment of that unique vision is our life's purpose and will bring about our highest material and spiritual fulfillment. When we are able to remember or contact our higher self we will be reminded of our life purpose, and we will be given the wisdom and power to create that future.

This is our quest — to contact and commune with the highest spiritual power, to ascend to the highest spiritual heights, and to use the wisdom and spiritual power that we gain to discover and create our unique personal vision, our highest life purpose. Then we have done our job. We have done what we came here to do.

Our material fulfillment is to commune with power and to discover and accomplish our mission in this incarnation. We all have a magnificent uniqueness — our life's purpose — something that we came here to do that the highest Power wants us to do. Each of us possesses the spiritual power to create this highest future for self and mankind. It's the power to become the best that we can possibly be with the highest wisdom and intelligence available. This is our path to real fulfillment, and when we use our power to discover and create our perfect future the universe will support us, and we cannot fail.

Love and Power are not like anything else. We have to give it away for it to grow, and we want it to grow and fill the earth. The emanation of the power that we are given is our flame of truth; it will ignite the hearts of others and the whole earth will become a paradise. Each person will understand his or her own life, what his or her purpose is, and how he or she is going to create it. As people fulfill themselves, the human race will be fulfilled.

Each of us has a compelling reason why we incarnated at this time. This reason is our purpose for this lifetime. Remembering and accomplishing this purpose is the greatest joy in anyone's life; this is what success is all about. What we have or don't have does not measure success and happiness. We can be rich and happy or rich and unhappy. We can be poor and happy or poor and unhappy. Success in life is determined by how we feel about our life. And how we feel about life is determined by what our life is about. The question is: "is your life about accomplishing your life's purpose?".

Successful people love what they do because what they do is an expression of their gifts and talents. Most people, when choosing a career, think in terms of money and status rather than thinking about what they are most suited to do. We each have a special gift, a special talent, to offer to the world. There is a distinction between career and vocation. A career is goal oriented while a vocation focuses on the purpose of our life.

Our purpose calls us to contribute our talents to work we love and believe in. Our career is important, but our purpose should guide and influence our choice of career. Career success is almost guaranteed when one is living and working from their purpose. People who put career ahead of purpose tend to be primarily concerned with upward mobility, advancement, money or some kind of material progress. This can lead to maneuvers that on the surface appear clever and smart, but often are manipulative, lack integrity and inevitably come back to haunt us.

Purpose is a compelling reason to live our lives with vigor. Our purpose is why we exist, it is an opportunity to contribute, to serve, to reach beyond ourselves and to make a difference in the world. Our purpose is always aligned with making the world a better place in which to live. Life is empty if we are not useful. We defy the primary purpose of our existence when we are not being useful. We abandon our gifts and talents and destroy the creative force within us when we are not being useful. We sacrifice peace of mind, grace, joy, happiness, fulfillment, self-actualization and contentment when we are not being used up. I like what George Bernard Shaw said:

> "This is the true joy in life, the being used for a purpose recognized by yourself as a mighty one; the being a force of nature instead of a feverish, selfish little clod of ailments and grievances complaining that the world will not devote itself to making you happy.
>
> I am of the opinion that my life belongs to the whole community and as long as I live it is my privilege to do for it whatever I can.
>
> I want to be thoroughly used up when I die, for the harder I work, the more I live. I rejoice in life for its own sake. Life is no brief candle to me. It is a sort of splendid torch which I have got a hold of for the moment, and I want to make it burn as brightly as possible before handing it on to future generations."

That is not to say that we should exhaust ourselves filling our days with meaningless activities. Rather it means understanding that we were created to fulfill a purpose and it is that purpose that empowers, inspires, and gives meaning to our lives. It is fundamentally important for growth, development and self-actualization that each individual finds the purpose for which they were created. For what purpose was I created? This is the most important question we must ask ourselves. This is a question that only you can answer, no one else can give you a sense of your purpose.

Remembering our purpose is more than a rational conclusion. It is instinctive and intuitive. The answer to the question "what is the purpose for your life?" requires searching beyond our mind into our heart and soul. One of the most fundamental things about purpose is that the fulfillment of it is in being of service to humanity. Life is at its very best when people are willing and happily contributing to each other. What distinguishes happy and successful people is that they are contributors. They are in love with life and all the possibilities of what it means to be human. Their accomplishments and their successes are rooted in their desire to grow and to be of service to humanity.

The idea of service and contribution is not new, but to many people the idea of serving connotes an inferior status. Albert Einstein implied that the only reason he found for human existence is that human beings are here for the sake and service of other human beings. We need to understand that our reward in life will be in direct proportion to the contribution we make. If we approach our work or vocation from the principle of service rather than for making money we will never have trouble with money again.

Apply this principle of service to your personal and professional relationships and you will be overwhelmed with the love, admiration and respect you receive from others. If we want to have a successful business focus our attention on the service we provide. Find something that is missing and needed and provide it — your prosperity will soar. When we have found the purpose for our life it is a fundamental thing that makes our life worthwhile no matter how grave the challenge, the situation or circumstance. As Fredrick Nietzsche said, "he who has a why to live can bear with any how".

The power of purpose can certainly bring you fame and fortune. However, the real treasure lies much more in how it enriches our life and the lives of others. The power of our purpose will help us access the only power that really matters: the confidence to move forward, to risk, to live the life we imagine for ourself with security that no matter what the obstacle along the way we know we can handle them. It is the power that emanates from the deepest part of us and there is not a human being alive within whom this power does not exist.

Now more than ever the world needs leaders. The world needs human beings who can inspire their fellow human beings with a fiery sense of mission. Our higher self knows our purpose. It knows why we are here. When our ego is not in alignment with our soul, we will not be able to perceive our purpose. Our higher self will constantly send us messages, circumstances and situations to help us remember our purpose, but our ego most times distorts the messages. Defining our mission is the process of tuning out this distortion and discovering what it is we truly want for our life.

The soul, the heart and the superconscious mind are where we can go to find our purpose and our mission. The soul is what pulls us towards a meaningful purpose for our lives. The heart shows us our true feelings about where we want to go and what we want to do. The creative mind focuses on the big picture thus helping us to rise above our fears and limitations. The process of coming to our mission in life is a solo event. It is something that we have to quietly go inside in meditation and discover on our own. Our higher self knows exactly why we are here at this time. It knows exactly what our purpose is and what we have to do. We will have to quiet our conscious mind, tune out all negative emotions and contact our higher self and request the answer to the question, "what is the reason for my being here?".

The pay-off for these efforts will be substantial; we will gain a new understanding and insight into why we exist. We will receive a precise and focused statement of our purpose in life, which will stand as a personal testament to what our life is about; it will be our own compelling mission.

When we define our mission we will suddenly begin to make connections, to see a pattern in our evolution as human beings. Our life will become less fragmented and more cohesive. What appears as separate unconnected experiences will gradually merge and blend creating a fascinating tapestry that is uniquely ours. This mission thus becomes our rock, a solid foundation upon which we can create the rest of our life. Who we are and what we do begins to fulfill an even higher purpose. Because of us the world becomes a better place in which to live.

When we live from the perspective of purpose and mission, we will find that we begin to love life. We begin to enjoy the process of life. We will wake up in the morning and will look forward to the day. People become very precious to us. We play life fully; we are at mid-field taking on all that life has to offer.

Some people live life as observers, they take no risks, they are watching from the sidelines. They are stimulated only by the fantasy of playing and then suddenly the game is over. The true players are at center field, they are playing with all their heart, soul, body and mind. That is the way we live when we have a vision and a purpose in life. We are at the center of life.

We become our main focus. Defining our mission implies choosing to get into the game. What position we play now becomes the important question. The answer lies in discovering where we are talented and how best to apply our talents.

People perform at their best when they are contributing their talents to something they believe in. At that time they find themselves being confident, enthusiastic, organized, relaxed, focused, in control, friendly and decisive. When people are not doing something they believe in they find themselves fearful, apathetic, messy, anxious, lacking direction, out of control, argumentative and frustrated. These people are not on purpose, or on mission and they find that their lives will not work.

The first step is to evaluate the special abilities you are good at. What do you find easy to do? What are your assets, what are your talents, what are your skills, and what are your major strengths? A good way to discover your purpose and your mission is to ask yourself, "how best can I contribute and serve my fellow human beings?". Ask yourself, "How would I like to be remembered?", "What do I dream of contributing to the world?", "What are my major contributions?", "What are my outstanding characteristics?", "What do I really want from my life?", "What would I be doing even if I weren't being paid to do it?". Think about these questions. Find a quiet place and just sit down and ponder on them. Close your eyes, get in a state of meditation and have your inner mind answer these questions.

These questions may require us to stretch our imagination. By defining our life's purpose we are choosing to live deliberately and not by accident. We are choosing to live consciously and not subconsciously. We are taking charge of our life in a way that has profound consequences. Defining our mission transcends any form of goal setting. Those are just stepping-stones on the path of life; our purpose is the path itself.

Once you have identified your purpose you can then organize a concise mission statement for your life. It can either be consistent with your present career or vocation or it can be something totally new that you got as the answer from you higher self. For example it could be that as an attorney you see a purpose as "I am helping people manage in a complicated world. My empathy and unique ability to simplify the difficult provides hope and encouragement to people". The return on an investment of energy and time you put into defining your mission is immeasurable; you will transform in the most positive sense how you feel about your life, your family and your world.

Vision

A vision is a realistic, credible, attractive future for your life. It is your articulation of a destination towards which your life should aim, a future that is important, a way that is better, more successful, and more desirable for your life than the present. There is an old Chinese proverb that says: "unless you change direction you are likely to arrive at where you are headed." Once you have defined your purpose and your mission, you are then ready to set the stage for a new vision. It is then time to focus on what you want and to turn your dreams into goals so that you are truly able to spend life in your own way.

The willingness to create a new vision is a statement of your belief in your potential. It is a bold declaration that you are in charge and taking responsibility for your life. It is giving yourself permission to dream once again of what could be and to believe that those dreams can come true. With a new vision you come to the future with positive anticipation rather than nervous apprehension. Most fundamentally, a new vision frees you from the limitations of the past and opens you up to fresh possibilities for your life. It is taking a stand against limiting thoughts and fears that prevent you from breaking through to new levels of achievement.

The fundamental thing that most people fail to grasp is how the principle of service works. Their lives are so consumed with getting rather than giving that they merely survive in a world of abundance. They get little because they give little. They get nothing because they give nothing. I hope you will now allow this principle to work for you, for you have gained the knowledge that reward follows service, so you are free to serve well. By remaining faithful to the principle you will be astonished by what eventually comes your way, for it is impartial, it plays no favorites. The principle of service does not value one contribution over another or prefers one reward to another. Eventually you will discover, like so many others, its generosity. For you will receive far in excess of what you have given.

It takes courage to create a new vision. The fear of failure is for many people an insurmountable obstacle to stepping out into an unknown future no matter how exciting and gratifying its promises. You must be willing to act even in the face of your fear. You cannot allow your fears to stop you. Fear is nothing but illusions and there is nothing to fear. In order to set a new vision for your life you must be willing to face all your shortcomings. You must be willing to face whatever it is that has stopped you in your life. You must be willing to be aware of all the obstacles in your life. You must be willing to see any barriers that have come in your life before and be willing to face them, to look at your problems and fears and to endeavor to pass them and to overcome them. You must be willing to conscientiously go into your subconscious mind and deprogram all limiting beliefs.

Your subconscious mind can literally be your best friend or your worst enemy. If you have any limiting beliefs which are unchallenged in your subconscious mind, no matter what kind of future you desire, if you don't deprogram these limiting beliefs they can in effect override your good intentions and keep you in a state of stagnation. Therefore, one needs to become conscious of all the limiting beliefs that one has and deprogram them. Then through the mechanisms of affirmation, visualization, concentration and substitution of thoughts, you can reprogram them in a very powerful and positive way. This is crucial for setting a new vision.

Another aspect of vision is that one needs to get very clear on what his or her values and desires are. Values form the foundation for vision. You must develop some clarity about what you value most in your life and the world. Get a blank sheet of paper and write down all your values and then rank them in order of importance. Once you are clear on your values endeavor to live by them. The test of values is whether they affect your action and behavior. Some primary values are love, trust, acceptance, respect, forgiveness, integrity, giving, producing your best at all times and in all service.

The mind attracts the physical representation of the image which you hold in your mind. It works by sub- consciously guiding you into the correct action to bring about the manifestation of your vision. A true vision must be holistic, it must be multifaceted, and it must include every area of your life. It must give you a balanced life so your goals will include not only those that involve career but it must include family, friends, health, mind, spirit and all dimensions of your life. Keep a journal and write down all your dreams for your life, all your wishes, all your hopes, and all your desired experiences.

As you meditate ask your higher self to clarify your vision. Whatever you perceive yourself doing just let your imagination and fantasy run wild; don't be limited by any thoughts of lack or scarcity. Remember that the universe is of value and that your life is prosperous. Imagine that you can have, do or be anything you want. Just write down what your innermost parts are telling you. Don't be frightened by it. Don't be alarmed of the complexity of it. Just write it down.

GOALS AND PROJECTS

Once you have defined your purpose and vision you then need to break it down into goals and projects. Goals and projects are specific steps to be accomplished along the path towards accomplishing your purpose. The fundamental thing is that your projects and goals must be congruent and in alignment with your purpose, vision and mission. It is not your purpose — it is just an elemental step towards your purpose. For example, you may need a house. Building a house may not be your purpose, it is but a project, but it may help you to accomplish your purpose. You may also need formal education. This is a goal, which may help you in accomplishing your purpose. Projects and goals must be specific. They must have a definite beginning, middle and end. When setting a goal you must have a date by which you are going to accomplish it. If you are not specific about your projects and goals then they are not really goals – they are wishful thinking.

A good example of this is my own case in writing this book. For years I have been talking about writing a book and not setting firm dates for when I was going to begin and when I was going to end, so I did not begin and therefore I did not end. Until one afternoon, after I had given a talk, a lady came up to me and said "You must write a book". I said to her "You know I have been saying that for the past three years, but I have been so busy doing other things". She said "Well this is the stuff that you talk about, you need to take your own medicine, set a date when you will start and when you will finish and see if what you talk about really works. I will even midwife the process for you".

"What is a midwife?" I asked. She said that a midwife is a person who walks a mother through the stages of having a baby. She continued "Consider your book project as a baby; once you have decided to write the book and start, you have become pregnant with the book. There will be a time when you will be excited about it and there will also be times when you will say I don't want to do this. But once you are committed you are already pregnant and there is no turning back. I will walk you through all those stages and make sure that you keep your commitments to yourself".

I said, "Great, lets go for it!" So, I set a date to start that very night and a completion date for two months. I was turning out a chapter every three or four days. I put everything I had into the project and worked long hours. There were setbacks of course; for example, my computer crashed and I could not locate the part locally. On one occasion I wrote an entire chapter and did not save it so I lost it. I was operating my legal practice at the time and had major trials going on. However, within three months the book was done. Don't be disheartened if you don't accomplish your project on the exact date you set for completion. One of the things I learned from college is that it is better to ask your professor for a short extension than to hand in a poor excuse for an assignment.

Nothing gets accomplished until you become committed. Commitment is one of the fundamental tools towards attaining authentic power and living out your full human potential. You can be dreaming, talking and desiring something for years and even decades, but until you begin realization of it nothing happens. You have to go through the process of deciding what you really want in your life and then commit to it and watch it manifest before your eyes. I like the poem by W. H. Murray, from the Scottish Himalayan Expedition, which goes like this:

"Until one is committed
there is hesitancy, the chance to draw back
always ineffectiveness.

> Concerning all acts of initiative and creation,
> there is one elementary truth,
> the ignorance of which kills countless ideas
> and splendid plans:
> that the moment one definitely commits oneself,
> then providence moves too.
> All sorts of things occur to help one
> that would never otherwise have occurred.
> A whole stream of events issues from the decision,
> raising in one's favor all manner
> of unforeseen incidents and meetings
> and material assistance,
> which no man could have dreamt
> would have come his way.
> I have learned a deep respect
> for one of Goethe's couplets:
> "Whatever you can do, or dream you can, begin it.
> Boldness has genius, power and magic in it."

In your journal write down all your dreams, hopes, desires and wishes that you would like to accomplish in your lifetime. At this stage don't hesitate, just write down all your dreams no matter how fanciful. Next dissect this list by taking out all the ones that you are most attracted to. Next, further dissect the second list by taking out only the ones that you are prepared to commit your time and energy to. Now eliminate all the fantasies from this process. Release and remove all the goals that do not capture your body, heart, mind and soul, no matter how grand. This is your goal list. To complete the process you then put them into categories of personal goals, career goals, family goals, and spiritual goals.

Once you have completed that list then distinguish them in one-month, six-month, one-year, three-year, five-year and ten-year goals. In the one-year goal, list all the goals that you have that you want to achieve within one year. Keep all the items in each category you would love to achieve. Be realistic as to the time frame so as to keep them believable. Goals should stretch you but not break you.

Enthusiasm for life is the spirit that will help you achieve your goals; it is activated by being involved with, and working towards, that which is meaningful to you. Clarity of intention and focus, propelled by enthusiasm is the most potent combination known to mankind. It is the genesis of all accomplishment; it is the key characteristic that bonds all those who take charge of their lives and set the course of their own future.

Make sure that your goals follow a specific format. Goals must have a beginning, middle and an end. Goals should also be simple, measurable, in the present (as if now), responsible and timed. There is a five step approach to setting goals called SMART (specific, measurable, all areas, responsible and timed) goals, which are very useful to ensure that you are on the right track.

S. M. A. R. T. GOALS

S **Specific**
    Simple
        Must be capable of being converted into specific assignments and targets.

M **Measurable**
    Meaningful
        Not abstractions
        Must derive from what our purpose is.

A **All Areas of Life**
    As if Now
        Must be multiple rather than single. To manage a business is to balance a variety of needs and goals. Goals are needed in all areas on which the success of your life depends.

R **Realistic**
    Responsible
        Must make possible concentration of resources and effort.

T **Timed**
    Toward what you want
        Must have time frames and deadlines.

CHAPTER 23

PROSPERITY

*True prosperity is to be successful in
accomplishing your life's purpose,
physically, mentally, emotionally and
spiritually.*

Why do some people seem to prosper while others don't? Why do some people seem to attract money and other material things to themselves, while others languish in poverty and impoverishment? When people have trouble attracting money or prosperity to themselves it is because they do not understand the nature or the principle of prosperity.

What is prosperity? Most people view prosperity only in terms of how much money one has, or how much material things one has acquired. While money and other material things are important and should not be undermined, it is only one small element of prosperity. True prosperity is to be successful in accomplishing your life's purpose, physically, mentally, emotionally and spiritually.

Prosperity is not measured by how much we have, but by how much we have succeeded in accomplishing our life's purpose and how we enjoy the process of life. It is fulfillment physically, mentally, emotionally and spiritually.

Prosperity is a matter of using the universal principles of existence and of using the techniques of the mind that we have already learned, to cause thoughts in our conscious mind to center on the idea of prosperity. We need to establish a deep understanding of the laws of prosperity, which is called a "prosperity consciousness". More importantly we need to live by these laws. The mind can be trained to think prosperously, in simple delightful ways. The results of prosperous thinking are deep and satisfying.

The opposite of a prosperity consciousness is a scarcity, impoverished or deficient consciousness. An impoverished consciousness inhibits the free flow of prosperity energy into our life. This can be disastrous.

There are some fundamental beliefs that one must have to facilitate a prosperity consciousness.

1. The Universe is Abundant

"Ask, and it shall be given you;
Seek, and ye shall find;
Knock, and it shall be opened unto you."

There is no lack or insufficiency in the universe. The universe is pure intelligence. It is comprised of energy and information. The universe is simply a large mind, similar to our mind. By learning how to use our mind and how to use the energy and information in the universe, we can manifest whatever we desire.

There is no lack in the universe. Scarcity is not a reality — it is an illusion, made real by the amount of energy and attention you give it. Why then, do so many people experience scarcity and lack? People perceive lack — because they are unaware that they, by their very thought process, create their own reality. Stories have been told of people who own and live on diamonds and yet live in abject poverty.

We can find a rich man with no money in his pocket and we can find a poor man with lots of money in his pocket. That is so, because it is not money that makes us rich or poor — it is your consciousness that makes you rich or poor. Stories have been told of people who win or inherit a lot of money and lose it in little or no time. The money will all flow to the rich man like iron dust is attracted to a strong magnet. The universe is abundant – it has every thing we need; however our consciousness operates like a magnet and can repel or attract what we want.

Some people do not see abundance around them and do not enjoy plenty. It is evident that they do not understand or do not apply the laws of prosperity. In their blindness they say that plenty does not exist, and so far as they can see, they may be right. But when they learn to see with their mind's eye, they will realize differently.

The secret of the law lies in one's consciousness. A man's life consists, not in the abundance of the things he possesses, but in the consciousness of that which he has. Man possesses the whole world and all its wealth, yet is only able to enjoy what his consciousness permits him to discern.

The thing we dare not do is to fret and worry about supply, or about where our next meal, or our next dollar will be coming from. Fretting and worrying restrict and limit the supply. They close off the supply and drag us deeper in doubt and fear. Instead of tightening up our thinking, we must relax and be more expansive. We must educate our minds to a larger state of thinking. When we can think and realize more abundance, we shall receive more abundantly.

2. The Universe Wants Us to Prosper

There is infinite abundance in nature. Nature supplies everything we need. If we live harmoniously with nature, we would understand that it abundantly supplies all that we need. Our only job is to recognize, understand and work with the laws of the universe.

It is important to believe that the universe wants us to prosper. The universe wants to see that we have sufficient and that we have the abundance that we desire. When we believe that the universe is friendly and working for our every good, we will begin to trust the universe. We will not resist or fight against life.

Many people view the universe as being unfriendly and therefore think that they have to resist it in every way. They resist poverty and deficiency and think that they have to fight against them. However, the more they resist and fight against poverty the more they create it. Resistance as a means of securing prosperity, peace and harmony is a mistaken and misleading idea. This is wrong thinking and only leads to disharmony and impoverishment. This is so, because our subconscious minds do not distinguish between desiring and resisting. It treats them in the same manner. Our subconscious mind is neutral and brings into reality whatever we are thinking.

If we go through life fighting, opposing, resisting and arguing, we are bound to meet with many obstacles and likely become so preoccupied fighting them, that we lose sight of our real objectives. If we are always getting ready for the obstacles we can definitely expect plenty of them. Rather, if we make little of the obstacles, keep our eyes and our minds on the prize we set out to gain, we will ultimately obtain our goals.

3. Prosperity Begins in the Mind.

Prosperity begins with an idea in the conscious mind. The universe is pure energy and information – pure intelligence – it responds to our state of mind. All prosperity is first produced by the human mind. Everything that exists in the physical world was first created in the internal world. All business endeavors are built on ideas. Before a business opens its doors and before any money flows in, there was an idea. Every endeavor begins in the mind. Therefore, all prosperity beings in the mind. Everything, no matter how big or small, must be created twice – first internally and then externally.

Working harder will not produce more money, nor will working more hours produce more money. Increasing prosperity requires changing your thought processes, so that they focus on prosperous thoughts. When prosperity flows into a person's life it is a direct result of the nature of the thoughts in his or her mind.

The way to think prosperously is to consciously change the quality of the ideas in our mind, so that the greater part of our nature is of a prosperous nature, instead of thinking about lack and scarcity.

By bringing about a positive change in our will, we will produce prosperity. By changing the way we think about money, we will change the way money flows in our life. In fact, just holding the ideas that "the universe wants you to prosper", "the universe is abundant", "the universe is supportive and there is prosperity for all", will create a consciousness of prosperity.

To be truly prosperous we must believe that there is abundance, and that there is enough for everyone, and that everyone should be prosperous. The idea of prosperity and sufficiency produces prosperity and sufficiency consciousness.

On the other hand, thoughts of scarcity, insufficiency and lack, produce deficiency consciousness, which produces self inflicted blocks that restrict the flow of prosperity and money to us.

The human mind is infinitely powerful. The human mind is of the same intelligence, which makes up the universe. Like the universe, the human mind is pure intelligence. You have this infinite power within you and at your command. Any thought that you do not have this power, will keep you from accessing and accepting it. When you believe that you do not have this power, it keeps you out of alignment with the universe and the universe cannot go to work for you in bringing your goals to reality.

The universe is exact and will always produce the result, exactly as your mind instructed. If your thinking is chaotic and out of alignment with your goals, your chaotic thinking will win out. Your goals will not be realized, because that is not the instruction your mind gave to the universe.

You must eliminate any thoughts that are not in alignment, or do not agree with the desired goal, outcome or state. Work on your thinking, use the universal laws and create thoughts that are congruent and in alignment with what you want.

4. Take Action

As long as we exist on this plane, taking action is a fundamental ingredient to success and prosperity. Many people fail to achieve their goals, because they fail to take action.

As we have seen, there are essentially two tendencies: the active or proactive tendency, and reflection or reactive tendency. People of the active tendency make things happen, they take action, they are the doer's of the world. They shape the world. When there is something to be done they do it. As the 'Nike' slogan goes "just do it". Proactive people look for what is missing and wanting and produce it.

Prosperous people create, initiate, and they act. While they are more likely to make mistakes, they are also more likely to do something, anything. On the other hand, an impoverished person will not act until forced to act. Rather than being active, they are reactive. Reactive people tend to study more than act. They let things take their course, instead of making things happen. Impoverished people are reactive types. They prefer to sit back and study things because they are not ready to jump right in until they have had a chance to fully analyze them. Most of the time they will sit back until they are forced to react. They do not get things done.

Reactive people will sometimes do detailed studies, evaluate the consequences fully, and react only when forced, saying "We don't want to do anything rash."

Success and prosperity are fundamentally dependent on your ability to take action. Whatever you dream of doing start now. **TAKE ACTION – JUST DO IT!**

Global Institute for Freedom Transformation and Enlightenment (GIFTE)

Committed to an Enlightened Civilization

Human beings have been given the GIFT of life.
The GIFT to grow, evolve, enlighten and transform.
The GIFT to be present in the moment - the here and now.
The GIFT to be co-creator with Source Energy.
The GIFT of at-one-ment - to unite with all beings.
and ultimately to unite with Source Itself.

What is GIFTE?

GIFTE is a learning institution whose aim is to promote freedom, enlightenment, transformation and prosperity.

Freedom is not only limited to physical liberty it refers to an unconditional release from psychological and spiritual prisons. To achieve freedom, GIFTE teaches that we must be courageous enough to depart from all the inculcations, indoctrinations and programming that have been entrenched into us by our parents, religions and cultures. When we have disengaged from all these entrapments we will be free and in exercising our freedom we become creators. We can create ourselves, create our being and create our consciousness. Only through freedom can we consciously participate in and experience the mystery of life.

By transformation we mean the ability to evolve, change and radically shift our thoughts, emotions, words and actions from a fear-based paradigm to love-based one. One of GIFTE's core beliefs is that transformation of behavior takes place when we confront our unconscious and work on our emotional and mental representations honestly and openly. GIFTE teaches that the Universe is abundant and wants us to prosper.

Enlightenment is the process by which we bring divine light into our being. It allows us to raise our consciousness from fear and separation to peace, love and unity, thus awakening from being a human machine to be a human being. The ultimate goal of enlightenment is self-mastery and complete mastery of this physical plane of existence.

Prosperity is measured by how much we have succeeded in accomplishing our life's purpose and how we enjoy the process of life. It is fulfillment; physically, mentally, emotionally and spiritually. The conscious evolution of the planet requires a shift from a consciousness of lack and limitation to one of unlimited abundance and prosperity. When we make this shift we will realize that there is no need to hoard, to fight or to go to war over property and possessions. For all that we need, will be abundantly provided. GIFTE teaches that we can have it all.

Purpose
The Global Institute for Freedom, Transformation and Enlightenment™(GIFTE) is purposefully designed to take you to the next level of evolution in your life. Our task is to demonstrate the superiority of present moment, life-centered and love-based awareness over an awareness clouded by fear. We work to shift human interest away from a defensive, survival oriented life toward the pursuit of excellence, enlightenment, empowerment and prosperity. GIFTE is for people interested in freedom, transformation, enlightenment and self-mastery, as well as people who have a desire to be leaders and role models of living a free, awakened and enlightened life.

Vision

The Vision of GIFTE is to build a global community of highly evolved and enlightened beings committed to raising the vibrational frequency of planet earth, thus bringing more love, peace, prosperity, unity and harmony into every aspect of our lives.

Mission

The mission of GIFTE is to achieve peace, love, prosperity and harmony around the world by engaging, leading and facilitating the personal transformation of people who have a desire to live an enlightened life through self-exploration, self-discovery and self-mastery.

Living By Conscious Design

Let's play together in the only game worth playing.
The game of discovering who we really are.
Are you ready for the next step in your evolution?
It's about time that we shift from a
fear-based civilization to a love-based civilization.

Be a part of the solution!
Heal your life and heal the world!

Living by Conscious Design is a trilogy of self empowerment programs dedicated to awakening us to recognize the GIFT of who we really are. It is a powerful and effective self-development series based on the simple truth that our context, beliefs and paradigms cause us to create and attract situations, circumstances and events that we experience as our lives.

Living by Conscious Design employs an experiential methodology. In a series of conversations and experiential exercises you will rediscover your true self and align your thoughts, emotions, words and actions with what you want to achieve. While conventional educational methods focus on content (adding facts, rules, or skills to your knowledge), the Living by Design methodology focuses on contexts and paradigms - the framework in which content exists.

The methodology cuts away our fears, negativity and limitations allowing us to create breakthroughs and extraordinary results in our lives.

THE TRILOGY

Part I: The Awakening

This 2-day program is about coming into consciousness. It awakens you from your unconscious sleep and allows you to take a conscious look at yourself. It turns on a light inside of you and you will never be the same.

Part II: The Clearing

This 3-day program takes you deeper into creating a clearing for your life. It focuses on deconstructing any remnant of the ego or inner child issues that prevent you from living the vision of your higher self. It calls you forth to choose life and to choose humanity and to recognize that we are all one. It leaves you powerfully clear and available to experience magic and miracles.

Part III: The Connection

This 3-day program connects you with your higher self and source energy. You totally grasp your powers of manifestation, magic and miracles. You recognize not only your power to affect your own life but also your power to affect the whole planet. At this level you become committed to the evolution and enlightenment of every being on the planet.

For further information and to register for one of our courses
Visit our website: www.mygifte.com
e-mail: info@mygifte.com
Or call us at:
647-347-6535 (Toronto)
876-946-1360-1 (Jamaica)

About the Author

Courtney A. Kazembe is the founder of the Global Institute for Freedom, Transformation and Enlightenment (GIFTE), an institution committed to an enlightened global civilization. He is an accomplished lawyer, entrepreneur, author, keynote speaker, spiritual teacher and a transformational coach.

For further information please visit:
The Global Institute For Freedom, Transformation and
Enlightenment (GIFTE)
www.mygifte.com
www.courtneykazembe.blogspot.com
You may email Courtney at: E-mail: Kazembe@yahoo.com
Tel: 647-347-6535, 876-946-1360